© Marietta Leung

STEPHANIE WU is an editor at *Town & Country*, covering culture, food, and travel. She is also the founder and editor in chief of *MochiMag.com*, an online publication for young Asian American women. She was raised in Taipei and now lives in New York City with a roommate.

HANYA YANAGIHARA lives in New York City.

THE ROOMMATES

THE ROOMMATES

TRUE TALES OF FRIENDSHIP, RIVALRY, ROMANCE, AND DISTURBINGLY CLOSE QUARTERS

Edited by STEPHANIE WU

Series Editor HANYA YANAGIHARA

PICADOR ■ NEW YORK

Printed in the United States of America. For information, address Picador, 175 Fifth Avenue, New York, N.Y. 10010.

www.picadorusa.com
www.twitter.com/picadorusa • www.facebook.com/picadorusa
picadorbookroom.tumblr.com

Picador® is a U.S. registered trademark and is used by St. Martin's Press under license from Pan Books Limited.

For book club information, please visit www.facebook.com/picadorbookclub or e-mail marketing@picadorusa.com.

Designed by Jonathan Bennett

Library of Congress Cataloging-in-Publication Data is available upon request.

ISBN 978-1-250-05145-5 (trade paperback)
ISBN 978-1-250-05146-2 (e-book)

Picador books may be purchased for educational, business, or promotional use. For information on bulk purchases, please contact Macmillan Corporate and Premium Sales Department at 1-800-221-7945, extension 5442, or write specialmarkets@macmillan.com.

First Edition: August 2014

10 9 8 7 6 5 4 3 2

To Ashley and Meera, the best roommates a girl could ask for

EDITOR'S NOTE

The names and identifying characteristics of some persons described in this book have been changed, as have some places and other details of events.

CONTENTS

Student Struggles

Adventures Abroad

Recent Grads

Young at Heart

INTRODUCTION

Over the course of my twenty-seven-year-old life, I've had about twenty roommates. Some—including my current one—have become my closest friends, who know more about me than anyone else; others have faded into the deep recesses of my memory, only to be dug up while browsing yearbooks and Facebook. And then there are the select few who are remembered by their eccentric habits as opposed to their names, like my camp roommate who stepped inside a wardrobe and closed the doors behind her every time she wanted to change.

As far as roommate experiences go, I've been on the lucky side. I've never had anything stolen from me or dealt with a mental health problem—that I know of. And after interviewing close to seventy people about their roommate experiences, it's clearer than ever that most people have at least one, if not two or three, crazy tales of cohabitation that they'll be sharing for the rest of their lives.

Whether for financial or social reasons, people prefer to live with others. The last time I had a chance to live alone (while studying abroad in Paris), I swapped out my university-assigned sterile studio for a cozy two-bedroom apartment with a friend. As much as I appreciate the ability to walk around naked, I'd rather come home to someone I can talk to and order delivery with. I'm not alone in this—in New York City, where I live, the number of people residing in nonfamily households increased by more than 40 percent from 2000 to 2010. Throughout America's biggest cities, rising rents and an increasing age of marriage have allowed people to embrace roommates (whether an old friend, a total stranger, or one's parents) long past college graduation and their early twenties.

It's no surprise that cohabitation breeds great stories—whether you're sharing a dorm with two beds within arm's reach of each other, a twenty-person summer home, or a thirty-foot RV. And pop culture has always been obsessed with the coming-of-age ritual of sharing a home with others: it's the entire premise for shows ranging from *The Golden Girls* and *Three's Company* to *Friends* and *New Girl*. In this book, you'll meet roommates who span from a nonrelative newborn child to a seventysomething with a proclivity for nudity.

Some of the stories in this book happened more than twenty years ago—before the 1996 debut of Craigslist, which has made finding new roommates easier than ever, and before the widespread use of cell phones and texting, which has greatly contributed to the ability to be passive-aggressive with said roommates. And then there are the thoroughly modern stories, made possible thanks to recent technological developments: college buddies who use their social networks to create start-ups from their apartments or roommates who abuse technology to commit identity fraud. There will always be boarding-school mean girls, hoarders, and those whose activities become questionable when they've had too much to drink, but I also discovered situations that seem rare but are becoming increasingly common, like dealing with a roommate with multiple personalities by attending therapy together, or the thirty-two-year-old Ph.D. who exchanges rent for cooking and running errands.

I couldn't be more thankful to the individuals who shared

their stories with me for this book. Some have been told so many times that the tales come easily to them; other conversations led people to remember roommates from their past who they'd long buried away. Some surprised me by tearing up when recalling their stories, a reminder of just how emotional and meaningful it can be to live, sleep, and eat in the same space as another person. One thing's for sure: living with a roommate is an incredibly universal ritual that we can all relate to—though some of my interviewees are so scarred they've vowed never to live with a stranger again. As highly personal as these stories are, together they paint a picture of a twenty-first-century household and how it's changing impossibly quickly.

—STEPHANIE WU

GROWING PAINS

THE CREATIVE BULLIES

I'VE HAD ABOUT THIRTY ROOMMATES—including three classically trained opera singers—but none of them were as horrible as my high school experience. In my junior and senior years, I went to a residential arts school to study creative writing. My roommate was a girl I'd met during a summer program, also for creative writing, at the same school. It was fine at first, but it didn't take too long for things to go really, really bad.

My school was a very isolated environment, with two hundred kids living under one roof. There were only about fifteen people in the creative writing department, and you saw everyone for hours every day. I can't remember when it all started falling apart, but suddenly, I was the target of a group of eight girls—and my roommate was one of the ringleaders. Art school kids aren't just mean, they're creatively mean. They're almost better at assessing your character and the things that will bother you than kids at a typical high school. I think they chose to bully me because I was easy to pick on—all my clothes matched, like a big pink blazer with matching pearl earrings. It was clear that I was bothered by their bullying and didn't stick up for myself. That made it more fun for them to torture me. They were mean to others as well, but I think my suffering was unique because of the close proximity.

The worst part was, I had to see these girls every day. It was especially hard during workshop time, because we writers were always sharing personal stories, and I knew they'd be able to use my stories against me. And my roommate was a compulsive liar—we took a poetry class and she told me that she made up things that had never happened to her. She once wrote a poem about how, when she was cast as a princess in elementary school, someone said, "How could there be a black princess?" Everyone else thought it was such a moving poem, but it was all made up.

The girls did things like taking an unflattering photo of me and setting it as the background on the school computers. When I went home for the weekend to see my parents, my roommate and her friends stole my food, slept in my bed, and went through my makeup. I found swipes of their fingers in my lip gloss and eyeshadow. They also started stealing things from me, like one shoe but not the other. They wore my clothing when they went downtown, and then took photos and put them on Myspace for me to see while I was home. When I was in the shower, they went on my computer and combed through my instant messages and sent them around to one another.

By the end of the semester, my mom was really upset. She spoke to the people in charge of residential life and told them my roommate was stealing and breaking my things. Their best suggestion was to take photos of my room before I left for the weekend, and they said, "If anything has been disturbed, we'll handle the situation when you get back." As soon as I went home, my roommate wrote on her LiveJournal, "It's too bad my horrible roommate's Bose speakers went missing." My mom read this and called the school, and of course the speakers hadn't been touched—they were messing around with me. I went to my writing teachers—in art school, they're almost like your parents because you see them so much—and they told me to tough it out. "Girls are mean sometimes," they said.

I remember they took my pads and taped them to the mirrors and wrote next to them, "What is this, a jumbo plane?" I had a sign of my name in my room, and they wrote swear words all over it. They stole at least a hundred dollars' worth of my stuff. I even spoke to a therapist a few times. At this point, all the friends I'd come to school with had teamed up with my roommate, so finally I decided to sleep on the floor of a friend's room until they moved me to a different room.

My problems with that group of girls persisted throughout senior year, but at least I had a different roommate by then. The girl who moved in with me was the first opera singer I lived with, and she acted like a diva, even though she was only fifteen. She got up at seven every morning and played one of two CDs, either Renée Fleming or John Mayer. I always woke up to her singing along. She was also very high maintenance—every night she painted her fingernails to match what she was wearing the next day. She had a portable bowl hair dryer that she sat under, wearing a gold brocade blazer and opera diva clothing. She bought her prom dress at a secondhand store for girls who can't afford expensive dresses. She lied and told them she couldn't afford a dress, and then bragged about how cheap it was. Of course she became friends with the group of mean girls, but she didn't go out of her way to make my life worse.

I don't know if there was one worst thing the girls did to me, but they had a huge effect on my overall confidence. Despite the fact that I knew what they were doing was mean and wrong, a part of me always wondered if it was my fault or if I was asking for it in some way. I still have moments where I'm very self-conscious because I'm wondering what people will think or say about me.

I've had a ton of crazy roommates since then—my college roommate listed her number one interest as Everclear, the drink, and named her fish Sushi. She liked to party a lot, and during the first week of classes started sleeping with a male cheerleader on our floor. One night they were having such rowdy sex that my friend in the next room over, who shared a wall with her, fell off his bed.

One summer in college, I did a homestay in France. That's where I had my second opera singer roommate—this huge, six-foot-three guy with bright blond hair. I assumed he was gay—he told me he was an opera major, he loved Kelly Clarkson, and he worked at Sephora—which partially explained the makeup I saw on his dresser and the fact that he wore mascara. When we climbed stairs, he said, "These stairs are working my thighs like a Hungarian shot put." Then one day he came into my room and said, "Hey, your friends are cute. Do they have boyfriends?" I was completely speechless.

I later studied abroad in Rome too, and lived with eight other girls in one huge apartment. These girls were overwhelming—they partied a lot harder than I ever did. One had a threesome in her room. One night, two of them came back and there was blood everywhere—apparently one of them had punched a taxi driver. They never cleaned or took out the trash, and left trash bags on our balcony. I went out there once to find it covered with maggots.

But none of them could ever compare to the mean girls. After all these experiences, I guess my tolerance is really high.

—M, 24 (F)

THE ENGLISH BOARDING SCHOOL

I WENT TO A PRETTY PRESTIGIOUS ALL-BOYS BOARDING SCHOOL in England for five years, starting when I was thirteen. It's a surreal situation to find yourself in. You're with all kinds of boys who have been mollycoddled by their mothers, including children of billionaires and aristocrats who've never had to look after themselves. One guy even had a bodyguard. There were a lot of students who were utterly incapable of survival in the real world.

At the boardinghouse, the older you got, the more private space you had. My first year, I was in a big room with nine other people. One guy in my room, Henry, was a huge tosser. He was disgusting and never washed his clothes. At thirteen, some of the boys were still prepubescent, and it's intimidating to share showers with eighteen-year-old men, especially when you don't have any pubic hair. Henry was resistant to the idea of a shower, which meant he stank. The smell coming out of his corner of the dormitory was unbelievable. We offered to wash his clothes for him, but that didn't make any difference whatsoever.

The other thing about living in a dorm is that you don't have any privacy. Teenage boys are going to masturbate, and one guy, Ken, was particularly obvious about it. The only place you could masturbate was after lights-out, in the dorm room or in a toilet stall. As you can imagine, it's not very dignified. Every night after the lights went out, we all talked for about an hour and everybody went to sleep. There was a bit of silence, and then we started to hear shuffling from Ken's corner of the room. It was horrendous. Everyone knew what was happening because of the audible sound effects—he had a little tub of Vaseline or something he used in the process. One night, someone replaced his tub with BP, a cream you rub on muscular aches. We all lay there in gleeful silence waiting, and sure enough, we heard the usual unscrewing of the pot. There was a thirty-second silence, and then Ken ran out of the room at high speed. I'm happy to say he stopped masturbating in the room after that. He must have known that we all knew, but never called us out on it because he was so embarrassed.

Then there was Jack, who was very obviously paranoid about the size of his penis. Everyone was convinced that before he showered, he had half a wank so that his penis was a bit bigger than usual. You could tell he was doing it because it was always at a different angle. It was terrible.

Yet another guy somehow managed to have sex with his girlfriend in his room, even though we weren't allowed any visitors. It was unbelievable and depressing, partly because most of us had never had a girlfriend in our entire lives. It's not a very nice way to live, but once you had your own bedroom it became more bearable.

I was quite a pretentious teenager—I had pictures of Bob Dylan on my wall and was desperately trying to imagine myself in a slightly more sophisticated life. And then I'd go to the bathroom and find that someone had taken a crap in the urinal. You couldn't escape the grossness.

The furniture was horrible too. In one of my semesters, I had a bed with a broken spring that poked out of the mattress. It was pretty sharp, and even though I turned the mattress over, it poked back through after a week. The maids and housemaster said they would replace it, but never did. I put towels on it, and for the rest of the semester slept carefully on my side at the edge of the bed—it's a habit I've had ever since.

There were about sixty people in each house, and you were paired with the same guys over and over again. Who you were roomed with was very important to the success of your year. I remember my last year in the dorm, when there were only five of us to a room, and smelly Henry was one of them. The older Henry got, the worse the smell got. His feet literally went green at one point. We confronted him all the time, but he got angry and defensive. He even got in trouble with the housemaster over it. And he's still kind of smelly and gross today, or at least he was the last time I saw him.

The school was stern about discipline, but students rebelled against it. Even at seventeen, you had an enforced bedtime. But invariably we found ways around that to sneak out. On Fridays and Saturdays, there were teachers whose job it was to go around to the pubs and make sure that if anyone from the school was drinking, they were legally old enough. Our nights out were punctuated with looking around and making sure that no members of the staff were around. Most of them hated it—they'd find one pub, sit there in the corner with a pint, and wait until their time was up. But a couple of teachers enjoyed it. We got a text message once when all of us were in a pub, saying that a teacher was spotted coming up the hill toward us. There was nowhere for us to go without being seen, and it would have meant real trouble if we got caught. So we all crowded into the toilet together and stood there in silence, hoping he wouldn't come in. I remember the door creaking open, and it not being him, but some random guy. He looked into the room, saw a dozen seventeen-year-olds holding their drinks in a tiny bathroom, and backed out immediately.

On Sundays, anyone with family nearby went home. The rest of us kicked around with nothing to do—the school didn't organize anything, so that meant many students got blind drunk every weekend without fail. It was a Christian school, so we had to go to chapel, but half the guys were swaying around, desperately trying not to fall over. A teacher always smelled people's breath to see if they were drunk.

Academically speaking, the school was great. After I graduated, I went to a university where you didn't have to have roommates. I was always very thankful not to go to an American university where you have to put a sock on the door if you have your girlfriend over. But there is something to be said about friendships like this, where I know everything about these guys. They're not necessarily my closest friends, but it's with them that I'm least on my guard, and most naturally myself—mainly because we know tons of hideously embarrassing things about one another.

—A, 30 (M)

THE TWENTY-YEAR FRIENDSHIP

THE FIRST TIME I LIVED AWAY from home was at a summer camp for gifted kids, also known as nerd camp. My first summer at camp was rough—I went from a public school that wasn't exactly known for its academics to an environment where I was no longer the smart kid—but my parents convinced me to go back. I met Dave my third summer at camp, and we hit it off immediately. I had shelves of comic books and he had shelves of Japanese manga, even though this was the mid-90s and manga hadn't taken off yet. Dave had lived in Japan for a couple of years, so we read each other's comic books—or at least, I read the ones that were translated after he explained that I should be reading them from the back forward. We convinced our RA, who was also a comic book fan, to organize a field trip to a local comic book store that wasn't too far from the campus. We also both loved Magic cards, which we weren't allowed to have on campus, so we hid them under our bed frames. And the two of us performed together in the annual talent show by acting out Weird Al songs with costumes and props.

Friendships among teenage boys are less sentimental and more, "Hey, let's do these things together." You spend a lot of time together because you want to do the same things. We had a running joke with this awful comic book I had that we were trying to get rid of. During the last week of one session, we kept stashing it in other people's rooms so they would have to take it home—it traveled from room to room, from floor mat to bed, and it was hilarious to see how widespread our joke became.

Dave and I saw each other for three weeks a year during camp for three summers straight. Our summer camp had a microcosm appeal to it—in three weeks, you cram in a full school year's worth of academics, which also feels like a year's worth of experiences. Time passes slowly—you think it'd blow by but it goes on forever. You can make a friend in the first or second day, and it feels like you've known each other for months. If you date a girl for three days, it's a big deal. I had so much fun at camp that I later worked there as a teaching assistant.

By the time our last summer rolled around, Dave's family had moved to Switzerland, so we were sending letters to each other with six stamps on them. We were competitive too—he once wrote me a letter on a piece of cardboard, which was cut up into a jigsaw puzzle. I couldn't top that, so I sent him a package of the worst comic books I could find.

As we both started to apply for colleges, my first choice was Princeton and my second was Columbia, and his were vice versa. Had one of us gotten into our second-choice schools, we probably would have been roommates in college too. When it came time for fall break, Dave wasn't planning on returning to Switzerland, so I invited him to my parents' home in Long Island. My mom went to a family-owned video rental shop to get us something to watch, and she said to the guy, "What would two teenage boys like? I want something like *Vampire Vixens from Venus*"—which, by the way, is a real movie. They found the movie and it wasn't until we were watching it in the living room that we both realized my mother had rented us soft-core porn. Dave and I spent a ton of breaks together, including Thanksgiving for all four years of college and most years since then.

After graduation, Dave spent a year teaching in Japan before returning to the States, and that's when we decided to become roommates once again. I did most of the apartment hunting, and we settled on Jersey City because the commute was easy and rent was reasonable. We shared an apartment for a year, until my then girlfriend (now wife) graduated and we wanted to move in together. Dave graciously stepped aside and moved to another apartment six blocks away. When I got married a year later, he was my best man. My wife and I are still living in the same apartment, and Dave's moved a couple of times since, but we've always been walking distance from each other. He's at my apartment at least once a week for game night. When my wife gave birth to our son, Dave was the first person allowed in the hospital to meet him. To some extent, you could call it a lifelong friendship—all because of nerd camp.

—C, 33 (M)

THE PUBLIC BACKSTABBING

THE SUMMER BEFORE MY JUNIOR YEAR of high school, I attended an all-girls precollege program. While moving in, I met my roommate Clara's mom before I met her. Her mom seemed friendly and told me that she hoped we could be friends. Clara was very quiet—whenever I tried to ask her a question, she gave straightforward answers and didn't open it up to any further conversation.

The two of us coexisted in peace. I played my music and did my homework, and she did whatever it was she was doing. As the summer went on, I began noticing more and more about her. She always wore the same navy tank top and khaki shorts with beat-up sneakers. I couldn't tell if she had a lot of navy tank tops and shorts or if she was wearing the same thing every day, so I peeked into her closet one day. There were only three hangers in there, holding three navy tank tops.

In the eight weeks we lived together, I never saw her do her laundry. She didn't shower a lot either. I often saw her pick at her skin, including her nails, acne scars, and scabs. I once caught her picking her toenails and eating them. It didn't bother me until I came home from class one day and saw her lying on my bed staring at the ceiling. When she saw me, she got up, and that was it. I didn't ask any questions and she didn't give me any explanation.

Clara and I weren't friends, but we also never fought. On the very last day of the program, we attended a banquet with more than a hundred people where students could share what they had worked on over the summer—there were a lot of monologues from actors and the creative writing kids. I wasn't paying attention when my roommate got on the stage, but I thought, "That's cool—I didn't even know she was a creative writer."

Then she started talking. "This is a monologue about my roommate," she said. I was not expecting that. "My roommate plays R & B music every single night. I hate my roommate. I hate R & B. I can't stand the music and want to kill myself. It makes me want to rip my hair out." She started talking about how annoying and loud my voice was, and how I stayed up much later than she did and always left the lights on. All my friends were looking at me, because they all knew who she was. The whole thing was totally confusing. I thought we had an okay relationship, and she had never once brought up the fact that she didn't like my music or said that I was too loud or annoying, and here she was, giving this very emotional public rant about me. Everything she said was hurtful, and much of it about my personality—she must have been keeping a list the whole time of things that bothered her.

That night back in the room with her was incredibly awkward, as was the following morning. We didn't talk about it—I couldn't even look at her. We both pretended nothing happened, and she didn't ask me what I thought of her speech. We both packed up and left, and that was that.

Clara was my first and last roommate. My freshman year of college, they asked me if I wanted a roommate and I said no way. It wasn't recommended, but they let me live alone throughout college. This happened six years ago, and I still get hyped up thinking about it. And I'm much more conscious now than before of how my voice sounds. Sometimes, when I hear myself talking, I'll wonder, "Does my voice sound annoying or loud?" Or if I play music, I'll ask people, "Are you okay with this kind of music?" Maybe she made me a more sensitive person, but it was a scarring experience.

—T, 23 (F)

THE BUNK BEDS

I'VE KNOWN JASON, my brother, since I was one and a half years old—that's when he was born. Our parents were studying to become professors and we moved to a different state every two or three years because of their jobs, and the two of us had to share a room. We had bunk beds as kids. I used to roll around in my sleep a lot and was afraid of falling off the top, so Jason got the top bunk and I had the bottom. The two of us were constantly up late talking and sharing stories. We were close as kids, though we had our fair share of fights and arguments, because we're both strong-willed people. Moving around so much forced us to get along, because we were always in a new community.

Sleeping in a bunk bed was exciting until we were in seventh and eighth grade—that was when we realized we wanted rooms of our own. When we had a big enough house, our parents gave us our own rooms. At first being in our own rooms was a little sad, but we got used to it quickly. When high school rolled around, I thought it was the end of my bunk bed days.

The two of us went to separate colleges. After I graduated, Jason was in New York working as a consultant and I lived in D.C., working first at the Department of Education and later in the White House. We first started Jubilee Project on the side to pursue a passion. We weren't trained in filmmaking but wanted to use videos to tell stories that inspire young people to do good in their communities. Over the next two years, we had weekly conference calls, filmed videos on the weekend on everything from antibullying to HIV awareness to sex trafficking, and posted them on YouTube. We've also done public service announcements, commercials, and recently, a short film with NBA player Jeremy Lin. We slowly built up a following, and after a few years, decided that it was something we should pursue full-time.

When you work in the White House, you get to have an exit meeting with the president. You can invite your family, but my parents had already met President Obama. I brought Jason; our third founder, Eric; and his girlfriend, Elaine. I thanked the president for the chance to work at the White House and we told him about the Jubilee Project. He thought it was a cool idea and told us he couldn't wait to see what we would do—it was an out-of-body experience. We left our jobs and drove across the country to California, because Eric's parents live in Irvine, and we moved in with them for a short time.

We started looking for a place of our own a few months later. By then we had some funds and a team of eight. We found a house with four bedrooms, and quickly realized we had to pair up. It made sense for Jason and me to live together again. We couldn't fit two beds in our room, so we got bunk beds for three of the rooms. Thankfully we found full-size beds instead of twin-size beds because we're both tall. And yes, Jason's still in the top bunk. The last room has a queen bed, because the two people sharing it are dating. Since we're a start-up, we're not yet able to pay salaries, but we do provide housing for the people who work with us.

We have a lot of house rules, primarily around chores and cleaning. Once a month, we all come together to clean the house, and Monday nights are for family dinners where we take turns cooking. Since the eight of us spend so much time with one another between working together, playing together, and sleeping in the same house, we've become a family of sorts. In the months we've been here, nothing has been too dramatic and we've all gotten along pretty well.

The best thing about living with my brother is he's even more clean and tidy than I am, which inspires me to be cleaner. After years of living in the same room as kids, we've learned how to creep into the room quietly. He used to wake me up all the time, but now he's mastered the art of getting into the top bunk quietly. We do joke about having girls around—he has a girlfriend, and bunk beds aren't the best situation. She comes over but doesn't spend the night.

The great thing about sharing a house together as a start-up is that you build a work culture. We try to spend time together and ask one another how they're doing in their personal lives, but also give one another space to have those personal lives. It wasn't planned this way, but everyone happens to be Christian, so we spend time praying together, which can help us stay grounded. I truly believe it translates into our work.

In an odd way, sharing a room with Jason as kids was a great foundation for what we have now. The only reason we can live together, work together, and have the same friends is because of all those years of living in bunk beds back in the day.

—EDDIE LEE, 28 (M),
COFOUNDER OF JUBILEE PROJECT

FRESHMAN YEAR

THE AMATEUR TAXIDERMIST

I FILLED OUT A ROOMMATE SURVEY before freshman year and was paired with a girl who introduced herself over e-mail as Alice. After a few exchanges, she started signing her e-mails "Kitten"—as in, "See you soon, Kitten." Shortly after, I found out that she wanted me to call her by this nickname. I can honestly say I never once called her Kitten; I always called her Alice. On move-in day, her parents called her Alice, but she asked professors and RAs to call her Kitten. She came from a strict family, was an only child, and was a super-talented design student—I think it was a persona she had decided to take on for college.

I knew from our first e-mail exchange that she was different. We talked about likes and dislikes, and she said things like "I really like dolls and dollhouses and little animals." That made me nervous. I was pretty shy and reserved about the whole thing and tried to keep an open mind, even though I knew we were totally different. I tried to embrace her weirdness as best I could.

One Saturday night, about a month into us living together, she decided to tell me that she was keeping a dead hamster—which had previously belonged to a friend—in our freezer. She told me she wanted to perform taxidermy on it and hang it in a hot air balloon in our room. This came as a shock—it was not the type of thing I'd expected to hear from my roommate.

I remember running to my friends and telling them, and they had a bigger reaction than I did. I was in denial that this was something I had to confront.

It took me a few days to get the courage to tell her I didn't want a dead hamster in my freezer. I was trying to be a good friend even though I disagreed with the whole thing. She asked me if seeing a real one would make me feel better, to which I said no. "I want you to respect the hamster," she said. "Would you respect your uncle if he died?" You can't compare the two, because I would never freeze my uncle in our dorm room and do taxidermy on him and hang him from a hot air balloon. The fact that I had to argue this point to her made me feel crazy. Finally, I got my RA involved. He tried to appease her and tell her she could perform taxidermy in a science lab, but she was not happy about it. The whole thing got shoved under a rug after a while, but they did have to change the rules at our school, one of the biggest universities in the country, from no animals allowed in dorms to no animals, dead or alive.

A few months later, my friend was joking around, and she said, "Let's check your freezer to see if there's a dead hamster in there." She opened the freezer and pulled out a dead fish. It was a goldfish that had been living in a little bowl in our room (fish were the only pets allowed). It must have died at some point, and I thought it was gone, but it turned up in our freezer.

Taxidermy wasn't something Alice had done before; it was a new obsession she loved. She also liked to collect things—there were a lot of stuffed animals and figurines and dolls sitting on her side of the room. I was a neat freak and her side was cluttered with all this crap she bought at antique stores.

Alice had a few other quirks too: She was also into burlesque vintage porn and wanted to hang up naked vintage posters of girls. She asked me to get rid of an Andy Warhol poster I had, and then tried to convince me to hang up naked

Dolly Parton photos instead. There was always something I had to say no to.

She was super obsessed with being skinny. She wore a corset at night and then measured her waist in the morning. She was super frail, and I'm pretty sure she only drank Ensure, the nutritional protein drink that gives you calories. Her burlesque obsession eventually turned into a hobby. Our sophomore year, after we weren't roommates anymore, my friend saw her performing at a strip club. I never saw her after we moved out. We didn't leave on bad terms, but it was like, *Good-bye. I'm not going to miss you.*

I don't know why I never thought about moving out. I guess at the time I didn't know what my options were. I was trying to make the most out of the living situation. Plus, if I didn't live with her, someone else would have had to, and no one would have liked living with her. I took one for the team in a way. I did make sure that the next year I didn't have to room with another stranger. My mom argued that I deserved a single, and the university gave one to me.

—C, 26 (F)

THE CLOSE-KNIT FAMILY

I STARTED COLLEGE IN THE LATE 2000S, when people were starting to find each other on Facebook and develop an initial impression based on social media first, as opposed to real life. My two freshman roommates were Jenna, a blond girl with a friendly, big voice, and Nicole, who had albums full of self-portraits on Facebook where she wore heavy makeup and was always brooding in dramatic ways.

I lived on an all-girls floor of our dorm, which was either called the brothel or the nunnery, depending on who lived there each year. The girls were catty to one another, so I stayed away from the social scene on our floor. I even joined the men's freshmen crew team so I could make male friends. But I did become very close with my roommates, and the three of us developed a dynamic that worked well. We didn't hang out outside of our room much, but we had fun together, appreciated one another's eccentricities, and got comfortable with one another. I used to vacuum all the time—I'm a bit neurotic with my cleanliness—and they always laughed at me.

I remember we had one bonding night where I realized that the two of them hadn't smoked pot or been high before, so I rolled them a joint. I got high and they didn't, because they weren't smoking right. So we decided to borrow a bowl from someone next door and we smoked out of the window. All the smoke blew right back into the room and hit the two of them, and they started coughing horrendously. Jenna had an asthma attack and I had to grab her inhaler; Nicole had tears of laughter rolling down her cheeks, and her black eye makeup was everywhere. They both got incredibly stoned and lay in their beds and didn't talk, even though I was stoned and chatty. As we got closer, we had bonding moments like that that we look back on and laugh at. We told one another about guys we were interested in or had been with and stories about class.

Nicole was relatively stable during our first semester, until she found out that her dad had been cheating on her mom for years, which led to her mom leaving her dad. And then her grandfather passed away—all within two weeks around Thanksgiving. Nicole started getting a bit depressed—she wasn't leaving her room much and was sleeping a lot and reading in bed with her lights off and a headlamp. She gained about twenty pounds—she was still a small person but seemed unhappy.

When Christmas break was over, we all came back and shared stories about what we'd done. And all of a sudden, Nicole said, "I have a story for you guys, but do you promise not to judge me?" "Yes, of course," we said, because that's always the answer to a question like that. And she said, "I've started seeing my uncle." She'd talked about how good-looking her uncle was after Thanksgiving, and we had written it off, since she was so quirky.

"What do you mean, your uncle?" we asked.

"He's my mom's younger brother and he's so hot," she said. "We're dating. We slept together, and he's amazing, and I know it's weird but I think we're soul mates. We've always had a connection."

Nicole started showing us pictures of him on Facebook. They'd gone on a trip and there were artsy pictures of them together, though nothing too suggestive. He was forty-five years old (she was eighteen). He was living the bachelor life and looked like he was trying hard to come off as young and hip.

After she left, Jenna and I looked at each other and doubled over laughing hysterically. We had no idea what to do with that information and didn't know what else to say. We felt pretty firmly that we weren't going to judge her, and we knew that she was going through a hard time. It wasn't really our place, but I did get her to go see a counselor in the health center. My mom is a therapist, and I've always liked having someone to talk to, especially a professional who knows how to listen and respond. I remember telling Nicole it was cool to have a shrink and convincing her to go talk to somebody. When I told my mom about Nicole, she pointed out that it was abuse, in a way, but didn't tell me it was my job to tell someone else about it.

The relationship lasted a couple of months—she used to Skype with her uncle in our room and giggle with him, and she introduced us to him. She truly believed they were meant to be together. Toward the end of the year, it fizzled out and she told us it was over. She later dated her best friend's older brother for a lot of college—maybe it was something about the intimacy of having a romantic relationship with someone who reminds you of someone you love. She was always looking to be cared for and for a father figure when hers had let her down. Since then, I've seen Facebook photos of her with her uncle during holidays, so it seems they maintained their close relationship. Whether it continued to be sexual, I don't know—and don't want to!

—L, 24 (F)

THE SECRET KEEPER

MY FRESHMAN YEAR ROOMMATE, Annie, was incredibly smart. She was fluent in three languages and so into physics and chemistry, and when she showed me her schedule during orientation week, it was full of classes like advanced organic chemistry—ones that freshmen technically aren't allowed to take. Most of us were taking four or five classes, but she was taking seven. She was also really, really quiet.

In the first few weeks of school, I wanted to go to Fashion's Night Out, and I brought her with me. I was so excited, because it was my first year in New York. She brought a textbook with her to read on the subway train downtown. When we got to SoHo, my friends and I were all sitting around a clothing store and sipping champagne, even though we were underage, and my roommate was in a corner reading her textbook. That was strange to me. Everyone at my school was a smart kid who worked hard, but she took it to another level.

For a while, I thought Annie and I could never bond. Sometimes we were both in the room studying, and she interrupted me to tell me something interesting she'd read in her textbook. I didn't have the advanced knowledge to understand what she was saying, and it was rare to meet someone who was so fascinated by what she was studying. I was so distracted by what was going on in New York that school was not that big of a priority for me.

That year, Halloween fell on a Friday. We all went out, but Annie went to the library to study and work on a research project. I watched everyone else around me bonding with his or her roommates and having a great time—we lived in the most social dorm, but Annie never wanted to hang out. I assumed she didn't want to make friends. I had a narrow view of her based on what I had seen.

Once, the guys on my floor decided to play a practical joke on us by putting condoms on our doorknobs. Annie freaked out—she had no idea what they were. She gave me the impression that she was a sheltered little girl who only ever thought about doing well in school.

One night, there was a storm, so no one wanted to go out. Our room was the biggest one on the floor, and the entire floor crammed into our room that night. We started out telling scary stories and bonding, drinking a little, and eating snacks. Then we started talking about what we wanted to do with our lives. We were freshmen who were getting to know one another—a lot of people said they wanted to be bankers or work for Google or go to law school.

When it was Annie's turn, she said she wanted to cure cancer. Someone very close to her in her family had died of cancer, and that made her want to devote her life to finding a cure. "I think there's a cure out there," she said. "We're just looking for it in the wrong direction." I thought it was so profound coming from an eighteen-year-old.

I waited until after the sleepover to tell her that I had been suffering from acute leukemia but was way too scared to tell anybody at college. And she responded by hugging me and telling me that I didn't have to pretend to be strong around her. It was so nice to have someone to confide in, and she became an anchor for me.

During the school year, I sometimes had to get bone marrow and blood tests, but was relatively fine. I was the first one in the dorm to be hospitalized, because I wasn't in the best physical state. I had been ill with the flu and went to the emergency room the third night of orientation week. Annie stayed with me then, even though we barely knew each other. She had seen me throw up a couple of times after treatments, but of course she didn't assume I was sick, just that I was some crazy party girl.

After we opened up to each other, our dynamic changed and we saw each other in a different way. She used to write messages on Post-its to motivate herself whenever she was frustrated by a physics problem, and I would roll my eyes. I later realized it was because she has this huge research goal that she's so obsessed with, and she wanted to become an oncologist and find a cure for cancer. I had thought that I was more mature and worldly than her, but she taught me so much about judging people and understanding that we all come from different places.

Annie never became my best friend, but I trust her much more than most people. She kept my secret for all of these years, and I admire that. There are very few people who are so passionate about a project that they're willing to give up their social lives. Some people want to be doctors because it's a stable way to make a living if you survive med school, but I don't think she's that kind of person. I truly believe she'll contribute to curing cancer someday.

—N, 23 (F)

THE GARBAGEMAN

BEFORE MY FRESHMAN YEAR STARTED, I'd chatted with my future roommate online and was looking forward to living with him. But a month or so before college started, he got word that one of his best friends from high school had gotten off the wait list and wanted to room with him. He asked me if we could switch roommates, and I said I was okay with it as long as I stayed on my floor. That's how I wound up with Blake. I tried to look him up on Facebook, but he wasn't on there, so we didn't connect until school started.

Blake seemed a little eccentric to me, and this may have partially been because I was coming from a foreign country and my understanding of an American college and its dynamics were all stereotypes out of movies. I expected someone friendly who I'd hit it off with. But from day one, I thought, *I don't know if I have much in common with this guy*. He was quiet and reserved, and we exchanged pleasantries and backstories, but never got each other's phone numbers. I lived with him for a whole year, and when we went our separate ways after freshman year, I still didn't have his number or e-mail. Clearly, we were never close.

The first weird incident I can remember happened in November, and that's what I like to call the ice cream disaster. A friend of mine, Doug, was trying to impress a girl on our floor, and had the genius idea of buying her ice cream in the middle of midterms because she was stressed. Blake had one of the only minifridges on our floor, so Doug asked if he could store the pint in our freezer for a couple of days over Thanksgiving break. Everyone was leaving for a few days, and in order to save energy, Blake decided to unplug all our appliances. When I came back, I noticed the fridge wasn't on, and of course the ice cream in the freezer was now soup. I had to call Doug and say, "Hey, that pint of ice cream is totally gone, so you're going to need a backup plan." I guess Blake unplugged the fridge whenever it wasn't in use, though I'm pretty sure you don't save energy by unplugging and replugging a minifridge. There were plenty of times when I turned on my desk lamp to find it wasn't working because he'd unplugged the entire power strip when he left the dorm. It wasn't just for weekends or holidays, it was a regular morning occurrence. That was when I realized he wasn't your typical college kid.

That incident was the beginning of a very passive-aggressive relationship. I'm certain I could have handled it better, but for two or three months, we didn't say more than a few words to each other, aside from hello when one of us walked into the room. We both studied in stone-cold silence and didn't exchange words for hours on end.

Blake had his fair share of interests and hobbies—I found out through friends that he was in an African dance troupe, which was cool because he was a white kid from the South. But his big passion was recycling: he hosted a dormwide information session on the topic and gave a speech about how we should all be recycling because there are bins provided in every room. But we were college kids, and it was one of those things where you might sort everything in your room, but then decide that the recycling bin outside the dorm was too far away and throw it all in the hallway garbage can instead.

After it was established that Blake was a bit of an oddball, my friends told me they saw him rooting through the trash and separating the recyclables from the garbage. It was bizarre, but I knew he was very environmentally friendly, so it didn't surprise me too much. A couple of days later, I came back to my dorm, opened the door, and saw a pile of recycling from the trash can in our room. He had turned our room into a holding dock for cans, bottles, and the like, before he went out and recycled it.

From then on, a little mountain of recyclables appeared in our room about once a week. Thankfully, it didn't smell, but I was disgusted. It was more psychological than anything else, that there was literally garbage in our room for a couple of days before he took it out to recycle.

One day, I was so fed up with Blake that I complained about him in a friend's room. He happened to be walking by and heard me, and he popped his head in and said, "If you have a problem, you can say something to me." After I apologized the next day, we went back to not speaking to each other. Our weird relationship allowed me to bond with the rest of my floor, including others who didn't like their roommates. I like to say it was fortuitous that I switched roommates instead of floors, because some of my best friends from college came from my floor.

I never did pick up Blake's recycling habit. It was great that he cared, but I wish he could've cared without bringing trash into the room. I'm a lot better about recycling now, maybe because I'm in my twenties and am more cognizant of things like that. Maybe Blake was ahead of his time—his heart was in the right place, but it just wasn't very well received by eighteen-year-old freshmen.

—A, 25 (M)

THE ALCOHOLIC GENIUS

MY ROOMMATE LARS was a first-generation prodigy from Eastern Europe. He had taken calculus in eighth grade and was taking graduate-level math courses as a freshman in college. He was very talented, but also had a clear and pronounced alcohol problem. He was so infrequently sober that it was hard to learn much about him. Lars was one of those individuals who, even in the middle of the day, cops would look at weirdly. He was six foot two, more than two hundred pounds, and had a shaved head. Whether it was intentional or not, he gave off a thuggish persona. In the short amount of time I knew him, he was kicked out of multiple dorms.

On the second day of college, we built a table so we could have a beer pong party in our room. He was standing on the table when it broke and made a loud sound. Two female RAs came running into our room to see what was going on. "We need your IDs," they said. And Lars started swearing at them, telling them to get out of our room. The RAs called security, who told Lars he needed to calm down. That's when he pulled his penis out, pointed it at the RAs, and screamed, "You're never going to get any of this, you ugly lesbians!" The RA who he was yelling at actually had to be restrained by the security guard because she was so incensed by what he was saying.

The next few infractions were minor—he was caught with alcohol a few times. Lars only lived with me for three weeks, but we spent a good amount of time together. Without a doubt, he was drunk more than he was sober. We heard crazy stories about him too—he was drunk in a graduate class once but managed to get twice as many questions right as anyone else. When he was forced to move out, I wasn't sad to see him go—I didn't want someone in my life who was putting my friends and me in direct danger.

Lars bounced around a few dorms after that, and in his final dorm before he was kicked out of housing completely, Lars's roommate was a quiet, introverted foreign exchange student with a computer science background. The RAs had told the new roommate, "If Lars does anything, let us know." So one day, Lars was in this new apartment, drinking before he went out. And the foreign exchange student went and told the RAs, who told Lars that he'd run out of chances and needed to find an apartment off-campus.

That evening, Lars went out and got drunk. When he got home, he saw his roommate sleeping and peed on his face. The poor kid woke up screaming and ran to the RAs, and Lars passed out not in his own bed but in his roommate's bed. He was woken up by security and kicked out of the apartment. He later told us he didn't even remember peeing on the guy's face, and that the security guards were actually laughing when they told him he needed to leave.

At this point, Lars wasn't allowed in any university housing at all. We still maintained a friendship with him, or maybe it was a fascination. And yes, it says a lot about my friends and me back then, that we decided to hang out with this guy after all that. Another friend decided to throw a party, and we gave Lars someone else's key card to get into the building. This was only about a month into the school year, and a lot of us had never seen cocaine before. He brought a lot of it with him and did it all himself. This party, like the other one, was broken up by RAs, and my friend who lived there tried to get people out of his room as quickly as possible—we all knew that Lars was risking expulsion by being there. The RAs were taking down names and figuring out who was there when Lars decided to get into the shower. As the RAs were about to leave, they heard the water running, and said, "Is someone in the shower?"

"Yeah, it's my roommate," said my friend. And his actual roommate—who hadn't been taking part in the debauchery—piped up and said, "No, that's not me. I'm right here." The RAs knocked on the door until it opened, and Lars came out in a towel. "We need to see ID," they said. Lars said he needed to get changed, went into the uninvolved roommate's room, put his clothes on, and somehow convinced him to let him borrow his ID. The RAs obviously knew it wasn't Lars's ID, and as he was fishing around in his wallet for his real ID, Lars walked toward the RAs, shouldered them so they fell to the ground, and then ran. Instead of taking the stairs, he took the elevator, and because the RAs were in complete shock, he managed to get on the elevator, which closed before they got there, and escape. I spoke to Lars a few times after that last party, but he dropped out of school soon after.

Among my group of friends, Lars is still a mythological creature. He was only around for four months or so, but eight years later, we still bring him up once in a while. In hindsight, I appreciate the entertainment.

—N, 26 (M)

THE PLANNED PARENTHOOD CHAPERONE

THE FIRST AND LAST TIME I've ever shared a bedroom with anyone was my freshman year of college. I was very into the indie punk rock scene at home and thought I'd meet a ton of other cool people when I moved to New York. My roommate, Anna, was a raver from a one-stoplight town in the South. I immediately knew we were very different people, but did want to try and get to know her because we were going to be roommates.

We'd been living together for two days when she suggested that we go dancing at Webster Hall, a club down the street. That was not my idea of a fun time, but I figured I'd entertain the idea, since I wanted to be open-minded and make friends. We pregamed in our apartment and walked down the block to the club. Webster Hall on ladies' night is the worst type of club scene—women get in for free, and the guys who come for the girls are gross and unsavory. I tried to have as good a time as I could. We got drunk, came home late, and went straight to bed.

I woke up at nine A.M. completely parched, went to get some water, and saw that Anna's bed was empty. I figured maybe I had been snoring or something and she had moved to the living room. Then I saw the dry-erase board with a note: "Went to a doctor's appointment, be back later. XO, A." I thought it was weird that she hadn't mentioned anything about waking up in a few hours when we were out partying until four A.M., but didn't think much of it. I went back to bed, and a few hours later, the landline in our dorm rang. I woke up to it ringing over and over again, and it was Anna on the other end. She sounded like shit, as if someone had punched her in the gut. I was half-asleep, but asked if she was okay. "I need you to come get me immediately," she said. "I'll tell you more when you get here." She gave me an address, which I plugged into Google Maps. I didn't have money for a cab, so I hustled as fast as I could on foot. As I came upon the address, I saw a giant Planned Parenthood sign and immediately knew what had happened.

When I saw Anna, she was limping a bit. She had called me because I was one of the only people she knew. Since she was put under anesthesia, she had to sign a paper saying that a chaperone would come pick her up, or they wouldn't release her. If they hadn't, she probably wouldn't even have called me and just come back alone.

I had invited friends to come visit that weekend—I wasn't exactly expecting my roommate to have an abortion the first week of school—and they were arriving that night. I offered to tell my friends not to come, since it was a sensitive time, but Anna didn't want to make a big deal out of it. "I feel fine," she said. "I don't want you to change your plans."

So my friends came, and we were all hanging out in the dorm room and drinking. I went downstairs to smoke a cigarette in the courtyard, and all of a sudden Anna ran past me and shot me a look of disdain. When I got back upstairs, my suitemate said, "What did you say? Anna says you told your friends what happened." And of course I hadn't. I would have admitted it if I had, but I felt it was so personal and not information that I should share with others.

I later confronted Anna, because I still had no idea what my friends might have said. She shut down completely and kept saying, "You know what you did. I'm not saying anything." My friends must have made some sort of joke that led Anna to think that I'd told them. I knew she was going through a tough time, but she refused to believe anything I said.

We had a contentious relationship for the rest of the year. I worked a full-time job since I didn't have any financial assistance from my parents, and every expense was a big expense. I bought my own groceries, and I had to confront her about eating my food. I couldn't afford to be feeding myself and someone else. She understood and was a bit embarrassed, but kept doing it. She did things like leaving eggshells in the garbage can with a piece of paper towel perfectly laid over them. We even fought over little things like whether or not there could be any dishes in the sink. Going into my sophomore year, I knew I could never share a bedroom with anyone else ever again.

—A, 28 (F)

THE IMPERSONATOR

BEFORE COLLEGE, I went on Facebook and joined a bunch of roommate search groups. I wanted to find a roommate I liked instead of getting a random placement. It was very much like online dating—I posted information about myself and cruised other people's profiles. That's how I met Serena. She seemed chill, and we both liked the same type of music. I'm half Filipino, and I thought one of the things I'd do in college was find my Filipino identity, and Serena was full Filipino. We talked about that and how we both wanted to keep eating Filipino food, and it seemed as if we had a lot in common.

The two of us agreed to live together, and were placed in a suite with three other girls. Serena, Alison, and I lived in one room, while Meredith and Lucy were in another. I remember feeling intimidated when I first got to college, but we all got along beautifully. I still have photos of us getting drunk and eating ice cream together on one of our first nights there. Serena, in particular, was super generous—she always bought us food and made sure everyone was having fun. We spent a ton of time together in the first few weeks. We even shopped at the same places and dressed similarly.

As time went on, Serena got closer to another roommate, Meredith, who was a writer, and suddenly started dressing like her and wearing glasses more. Later, she got close to Lucy, who was more of a hipster, and did the same thing. It seemed as if Serena adjusted her wardrobe based on who she was hanging out with most.

We were careless freshmen, and at one point, we noticed that money was often missing from our wallets in the morning, but didn't think much of it. We figured we'd spent it when we were drunk. Serena and I stayed close, but I started dating a guy and spent a lot of time with him, so I wasn't hanging around the room as much.

One Monday, I got back from a weekend away and was walking around campus without my wallet. That afternoon, Serena texted me to say that she had found my debit card in the quad. At that time, I wasn't thinking about the fact that I hadn't brought my things out with me. But when she brought the card to me, it was beat up and looked like it had been messed with, so I had to get a new debit card. Later that week, I needed to make a copy of my driver's license for my internship. I had a fake ID at the time, which was the one I kept in the front of my wallet. When I went to dig for my real ID, it wasn't there.

I called my boyfriend to tell him what had happened, and he told me that considering my card was stolen earlier in the week and that my ID was missing, I needed to file a report. "You need to check your bank account," he said. I was never good with money. I only ever had a hundred dollars or so in my bank account at once, and if I ever ran out, my parents were happy to spot me fifty dollars. When I logged on to my bank account, I was four thousand dollars in the red. I called my bank immediately, and they said they'd get back to me with more information. Meanwhile I went to the police station, and Serena came with me—I was inconsolable, and she bought me ice cream to make me feel better.

I filed an identity theft report, and back at our apartment, everyone was on edge. Two days later, my bank confirmed that someone had gone to the bank and pretended to be me. That's when I realized it wasn't just someone stealing my money—I was actually being impersonated. I checked my account again, and someone had tried to deposit a four-thousand-dollar check into it, which had been flagged for unusual activity. Later, Alison, the other girl in my room, came up to me and said, "You know that check that was cashed into your account? It was mine." And she showed me a copy of a blank check that her parents had given her for enrollment fees. We saw that someone had written on the check that four thousand dollars was to be paid out to me for babysitting.

This was even more terrifying, because not only had someone been in our apartment to steal the check but they also knew that I was a babysitter and thought they'd be able to get away with writing that on a check. During this time, I was in touch with a detective at the police station, who kept asking if there was anyone in my life who might be trying to hurt me, but there was no one I could think of. The detective was also trying to get his hands on security camera footage from the bank to see who had gone into the bank that day pretending to be me.

All this was happening during finals week, and as I was writing a paper, I got a message from the police station saying the footage was in and I should come down to take a look at it. I went back to my room and told my roommates that I was going to see the footage later so we could finally get to the bottom of everything. As I was finishing up my paper, I got a text from Serena. "Oh my god," she said. "You're finally going to figure out who it is, I wonder who it will be." She also told me that Alison was going to the police station later to talk about her check, so maybe we should go together. I thought that was a good idea, and told the detective I was coming with Alison around three P.M. "No," he said. "Come by yourself."

I told Serena and Alison the police wanted to talk to me alone, and I was working on my paper when I got a call from an unknown number. I picked it up and a weird-sounding voice said, "Hi, we're calling from the precinct. The detective is sick right now and can't see you, so don't worry about coming in today. Do you have this number to call back if you have any questions?" And I remember saying, "Yes, you called my cell phone, so I have the number saved."

I hung up and thought it was a weird call, so I went on the precinct Web site to see if any of the listed numbers matched the one that called me, but it was a completely different area code. That's when I called the detective myself to ask if someone from his office had called to tell me not to come in, and was met with dead silence. "No," he said. "Someone doesn't want you to be here right now, and you need to come here without telling anyone what you're doing."

I went back into my room and slipped my books under my bedsheets so people would think I was still in the library. Thankfully, no one was there. As I was taking the stairs down, I bumped into Serena in the stairwell. She started speaking, and I had a sinking realization that she was the one who had called me on the phone. I freaked out and ran away, but then had a moment of doubt—was I insane to be accusing Serena? I went back and apologized, and she asked where I was headed. I told her I was turning in my paper, and she offered to come with me, but I made up an excuse to go alone.

I'm bad with directions and was on the phone with my boyfriend while trying to get to the precinct. I made a huge loop, and while I was on the phone, I got two more calls from the mysterious number that had called me before, plus a text from Serena saying she was in the library. Twenty minutes later, I was approaching the police station and could clearly see her standing across the street. I freaked out and ducked into a shop on a side street and called the detective again. “My roommate is outside,” I said. “I think she has something to do with my identity being stolen.” The detective told me they had her in custody—they spotted her walking around outside and recognized her from the bank footage. I asked the police to send an escort because I was so scared. When I got to the station, I told them I didn’t want to see Serena. They showed me the security tapes, and sure enough, it was Serena at the bank, in an outfit I’d helped her pick out. Then the detective asked if I called the police station saying my boyfriend had broken up with me and my computer had crashed and that I couldn’t come in today, which I clearly hadn’t. Serena had been impersonating me and the police using fake phone calls the whole time.

She went to jail that night and was charged with four felonies: grand larceny, impersonation of a cop, possession of forged documents, and identity theft. She had gone to the bank that day to get another debit card in my name using my ID. We don’t look anything alike, so they must not have looked at it very closely.

The next morning, Alison found out that all the calls and e-mails she’d been getting from the police were actually from Serena too. She thought she was communicating with a detective the whole time, but never was. Serena called me the next day after she was released, crying, and said, “I’m so sorry, I want to let you know this is the only time I’ve stolen from you.” It sounded like something her lawyer had told her to say. She went back to the apartment with her parents, didn’t look at anyone, took a few things, and dropped out of school that day. Later that week, she sent a long Facebook message to our good friends, a clichéd message about how she was just a girl who had gotten in over her head. She had an entire story about how she’d been dealing with drug addiction since high school and had taken my money because she knew the bank would give it back to me and her cocaine dealer would hurt her if she didn’t pay him. I knew the story was fake, because my friends told me she'd only started doing coke recently and was obsessed with it. It was as if she knew she needed a story for cover.

Since then, none of us have heard from Serena. I heard she got off with community service and didn't have to spend any time in jail, because of her drug addiction story. The scariest thing was the way she cloned herself into the people she was hanging out with—it was as if she never had an identity of her own.

—V, 24 (F)

STUDENT STRUGGLES

THE ELEVEN-WOMAN SUITE

I'VE HAD MORE THAN THIRTY-FIVE ROOMMATES, including a gay video gamer who never left his bedroom—he was constantly playing World of Warcraft and having Craigslist hookups in the middle of the night. The biggest contribution to my number of roommates was when I lived in an eleven-person suite two years in a row in college. I chose the suite because it was low-cost and allowed smoking. I figured that the type of people who wanted to live in a smoking apartment were people who liked to have fun. If a few people each had one friend over on a Friday night, it turned into a huge party. We had all come in as random roommates but formed a real bond, with the exception of Michelle, an alcoholic with a serious eating disorder. I think it was genetic—her brother was an addict too.

Michelle weighed about ninety pounds, only ate boiled chicken and broccoli, and went straight to the bathroom after she ate. Once she passed out in the bathroom with the door locked and the water running, and we had to break the door down. When the girl who shared her room found laxatives under Michelle's bed, we knew we had to confront her, but nobody knew the right way to do it.

One day, she busted her two front teeth on the pavement while wasted. After she came back with her teeth knocked out and blood all over her shirt, we told her that she had a problem. She slammed the door in our faces and refused to talk to us. It didn't help that her mother was an enabler who had bought her porn-star breast implants as a high school graduation gift. She called her mother the next day for emergency dental work, lied about what happened, and said she fell on the stairs. Her mom sued our school and essentially made back what they paid in tuition.

The next year of college, six of us stayed together, but the other rooms were filled with even more characters. One was a conservative Jewish girl, and she always stirred up some sort of war about having the lights and the oven on while she was observing the Sabbath. Whenever anyone came over, it turned into a very intense political conversation about Israel and Palestine.

But no one can quite compare to the roommate we nicknamed Hooky. She was into some bizarre things, like suspension on hooks. Some people are into it as an erotic thing, but to me it's a form of masochism. Hooky went to parties and BDSM conventions where people get together and hang from the ceiling on hooks and swing.

Hooky kept to herself most of the time. There was a time during finals when no one saw her for a long period, and we all texted to ask if she was okay. I thought maybe she had gone home to Westchester, but one day I came home to her casually smoking cigarettes in our living room area, like she'd been there all along. "Where've you been?" I asked. "No one's seen you in ages." She told me she'd gotten depressed, hadn't left her room in a month, and then went to a doctor who gave her medicine for schizophrenia. "Now I feel great," she said.

The guys she brought over were weird too—one had a split tongue, and another had implants under his skin so it looked like he had lizard bumps. She also had hooks in her bedroom. We told her she wasn't allowed to hang in her room, but she said she couldn't anyway because the hooks were too low. The hooks were more display items she had for shock value. Living in the suite honestly felt like *The Real World* with only women.

—A, 30 (F)

THE OBSESSIVE LESBIAN

MY SOPHOMORE YEAR OF COLLEGE, I was looking to move out of my apartment because my two roommates, a guy and a girl, had become a couple. They started hooking up about a week after moving in together, and I figured it wasn't any of my business. But the way we handled the roommate affairs was that each of us voted on everything. And when they became a couple, they started voting as a block, because they didn't want to make the other one mad. So when I didn't want to get cable because I wasn't home that much to watch it, they said, "We're both for it, so you have to pay for it." We used to take turns buying household supplies, and they took a turn as a couple and then it was my turn. It went quickly from we're going to be great roommates to I have to get out of here. I felt like I was in their relationship, and it was a nightmare scenario.

A guy I studied abroad with said he was moving out of a two-bedroom, and his female roommate went to a different college but was in the same city. He said she was a nice person, but he was a neat freak and she was a little too messy. "How messy are we talking?" I asked. And he told me how she threw her keys on the table, or left her jacket on the couch instead of hanging it up. To me, that's not messy. I thought he was sort of anal-retentive. Little did I know, he was just trying to say anything he could to get out of there, because she was such a terrible roommate. I went to visit the apartment, and it was all decorated from Pier 1, very world-art themed. It was in a cute old building, a Victorian house that was subdivided into apartments. She seemed perfectly nice—she was a very polite southern girl with a thick accent. It seemed like a great arrangement, and we both knew we weren't going to become best friends.

I soon started noticing that she lied to me a lot. I often came home to find the apartment reeking of smoke, as if someone had been smoking in the living room. When I asked if she'd been smoking, she said, "No, it came in from outside, I'd never smoke in here." And she did typical bad roommate stuff, like eating my food out of the fridge and using all my shampoo. Whenever I asked her about it, she said, "I don't know what you're talking about." It was annoying, but not a huge deal.

Then one day, things got weird. I came home and she'd left her diary in front of my bedroom door. The diary was open on a passage about how she was questioning her sexuality and she wasn't sure if she had feelings for me or her male best friend. And I thought, *If she wants to have a conversation with me about this stuff, I'm happy to talk to her about it, but what a weird way to go about it.* So I closed her diary and put it back near her room, and didn't say anything about it. Then she started leaving these weird little sculptures in front of my bedroom, made out of pieces of paper she'd gotten out of my bedroom trash, like a letter from my mom or a birthday card I'd thrown away after a few weeks. She took these pieces of paper and folded them into origami and piled them up into a sculpture and never said anything about it. Sometimes my clothes or CDs went missing, and a mutual friend told me she was wearing my clothes out, and rotated them and then put them back in my closet, hopefully before I saw they were gone.

Then I started noticing that she was coming into my room

when I was asleep. We were not best friends, or nearly close enough for this to be a normal thing. When I woke up in the morning, things that I knew for a fact had been in my room when I went to bed were now in the living room. She had come in while I was asleep and took my cordless phone off its cradle and left it in the living room, though we also had a landline out there. It was a little creepy, and I dealt with it by spending more time on campus during the day and nights with my boyfriend. Sometimes I came home from his house and my sheets were all rumpled, as if someone had slept in my bed, and it smelled like cigarettes. But my roommate said no one had been in my room, though she had clearly been sleeping in my bed or letting someone else sleep there.

I thought of trying to lock my room, but I had one of those doorknobs that could only be locked from the inside, because there was no key. One time I had locked the door and I heard noises that sounded like the doorknob jiggling. I opened the door quickly, and my roommate was standing there with a penny that she was trying to place in the slit and turn it like you would with a key. "I was looking for something and thought maybe it fell out and got into your room somehow," she said. After that, I never truly felt like my things were secure.

At this point, the weirdest thing she'd done was leave a pair of underwear that she'd had her period in on the living room floor. Then one day, I asked her about something else of mine that had gone missing. She denied it and said I was being weird. When I came home later, on the front door of our apartment building was a page from a catalog I'd thrown out, with all these mean things about me written on it, as if I was the girl from the catalog picture. She wrote stupid things, like "I think I'm a feminist but I spend every night at my boyfriend's house," "I spend too much money on clothes and won't share my food with anybody," and "I'm a bitch and everyone hates me"—nasty things she thought were true of me. And she'd crossed out the girl's eyes, like you would do to a dead person, and drew a pentagram on her forehead.

That's when I decided I'd had it. I'd tried to have conversations with her about everything that was happening, but she denied it all. It almost felt like a multiple personality thing, where I was dealing with two people—one was a prim and proper southerner, and the other was a crazy person who was always acting out. Whenever I tried to talk to her, I got the buttoned-up one who always said, "I don't know what you're speaking of, that's disgusting." The note on the door was the last straw. I called my boyfriend, and he came over and kept me company while I put everything in garbage bags and moved into his house. And I never went back. I still paid rent to the landlord, but I didn't do anything that necessitated us staying in touch. And I do feel like she knew she'd done something wrong, because if you thought you had a fairly normal roommate relationship, and then you came home one day and all your roommate's things were gone and she'd moved out without a word, you'd text them or ask if something had happened. But I never heard from her again.

Afterward, I lived with my best friend, which went great. And I decided I'd had too many bad experiences living with strangers, so unless I could live with my best friend in the world, I was going to live by myself. Even when I moved to New York, where most people have roommates, I did whatever it took to save enough money to live alone, whether it was taking a second job or never going out for dinner. My only roommate in the past ten years has been my dog.

—S, 32 (F)

THE PARTY POOPERS

I WENT TO BOSTON COLLEGE, where the housing system is lottery-based and you need to find a certain number of roommates to fit a lottery slot. It's a very dramatic situation that can ruin friendships. As seniors, everyone wants to live in the Modulars, a group of dorms that is the hub of the party circuit on campus. You need six people to apply for an apartment, but it's the most desirable place to live because you have a huge yard, or Mod Quad, which you share with about forty other people. I was studying abroad while we were applying, and some of our friends had decided to group together without telling the rest of us. So in order to apply for the Mod, my best friend, Mandy, and I joined up with Nina, a good friend from abroad who had a group of four.

We got an apartment at the Mod, which was exciting, because the friends who screwed us over didn't. When it came time to move in, Mandy and I quickly realized we weren't on the same page as these other girls. We wanted to live in the Mod because it was a party area, and if you live there, it's assumed that you're okay with people up at all hours, any day of the week, and that you'll be throwing your own parties. But any time Mandy and I wanted to have people over, it was a knock-down, drag-out brawl. The other four girls never wanted to contribute to alcohol or food or clean up or set up, and then at the eleventh hour, their friends all showed up first and drank our beer before our friends got there.

We threw a huge Christmas party, and I spent hundreds of dollars getting tons of drinks, food, and even an ice luge. The day of the party, one roommate, Angie, showed up with her soccer team after telling me she wasn't willing to contribute more than twenty dollars. And then the other roommates complained throughout the following week about how we didn't clean up quickly enough, and that we were loud, and people were there late.

On St. Patrick's Day, we threw a Kegs and Eggs party so we could drink and have some food in our stomachs before we went out. A friend of Mandy's and mine got too drunk and had to be dragged into our shower and hosed off, because he had somehow rolled in mud. I didn't even know he was there, and when I found out, I kicked him out because he was way too drunk. A couple of days later, one of the roommates sent a text to the group, saying, "When is the disgusting mud going to be cleaned out of the shower from your friend on St. Patrick's Day?" Our Mod had two showers, and I never used the other one. I'd already cleaned the entire apartment after our party, and had I known the shower I never used was dirty, I would have cleaned it too. But they were telling me they'd showered in two inches of mud for four days before passive-aggressively saying anything. I didn't even feel bad for them.

In April, the Boston Marathon rolled around. BC is located at mile twenty-one, right after Heartbreak Hill, the hardest part of the marathon. The school encourages people to cheer marathon runners on and have a great time. We wanted to throw a party, but our roommates were hesitant and didn't want to be involved. Which was fine—we told them, if you don't want to be around, go somewhere else. We got money from another group of kids to throw the largest party in the Mod, and we had tons of food, jungle juice, and beer. Angie showed up with her friends again and drank our beer and ate our food, but the marathon was such a happy event that we brushed it aside.

The bombings happened later that afternoon. Mandy and I cleaned up the party, like we always did, with no help. The rest of the week in Boston was bizarre—the bombers were on the loose, and no one knew what was going on. On Thursday night, we were out in Boston and got an emergency text message saying that the suspects were driving on a road toward BC from downtown Boston, and that they were throwing bombs out the window and an MIT officer was dead.

My friends and I knew we weren't going to take a cab from downtown in the same direction as the bombers, so nine of us spent the night at a hotel where a friend's parents had a timeshare. The next day, the entire city was on lockdown. Everyone on campus was given fifteen-minute time slots where they could be escorted to dining halls. We were downtown the whole time, so when the younger bomber was apprehended three miles from BC, the city erupted into a huge party. We made our way back to campus and were celebrating at a bar when we started receiving text messages that there was a huge party of four hundred people in our Mod Quad, with some waving American flags out the windows and blasting music across the yard.

This sounded awesome, so we got back on the bus, where everyone was singing "Sweet Caroline" and "The Star-Spangled Banner" and going absolutely nuts. People were walking in and out of our Mod, mostly friends of ours who needed to use the bathroom. The police broke up the celebration around two thirty in the morning, and we were still standing around, watching the crowd disperse. We'd never seen anything like it before.

At some point in the night, our roommates had decided to lock our doors. So every time we wanted to go inside for something, or let one of our good friends into the bathroom, we had to pound on the door. Two roommates kept saying we were waking them up, even though there were four hundred people in the yard and school had been canceled the next day. Two of my friends had passed out in our apartment, and one roommate decided to wake them up and kick them out. We eventually got into a huge fight—Nina slammed the door in our faces, then cried about how mean we were being, even though she was the one who had locked us out of our own dorm.

The next day, things were obviously awkward. We were pulled into a roommate meeting and accused of throwing a party without telling anyone or allowing them to invite their friends. They said we had let things get out of hand, as if we had invited the entire population of BC into our yard, even though we had been downtown for the whole thing and arrived when it was already under way. It was the type of blowout that happens after the World Series, or after Osama was captured, and they blamed the entire party on us because it happened in our yard.

When the year ended, three girls booked it without cleaning up—my parents and I stuck around until late at night cleaning up the apartment. I honestly think my roommates were sour people who were unhappy for some reason, and we were easy targets because we liked to have fun. I still had a great senior year, but living in the Mod with people who didn't ever want to entertain was really difficult. At BC, if you're lucky enough to get one of those apartments, it's your duty as a senior to entertain.

—Z, 24 (F)

THE OVEREXCITED BLADDER

I FIRST MET NANCY my sophomore year of college, and that summer, we lived with a few other girls on campus while taking classes. Nancy and I got along very well, so when both our fall housing arrangements fell through, we decided to continue living together. The two of us shared a very small off-campus apartment, with two bedrooms and one bathroom.

As we were moving in, she told me an embarrassing story that had happened on her birthday. "I was making out with a guy," she said. "But I drank too much and peed on myself." Thankfully, she had a small bladder, so it looked like she'd been sweating a lot.

I'd seen Nancy drink before, but she was always fine. I don't know if it was a combination of drinking and stress, since it was right around the Thanksgiving holiday, but I woke up early one morning and was heading to the bathroom barefoot when my feet hit a wet spot on the hallway carpet. *That's weird,* I thought. *Our walls must be leaking.* The apartment was ratty—I woke up one morning with plaster on my bed. I went to the bathroom and came back out, and realized the wet spot smelled kind of funny, but ignored it.

When Nancy woke up, I told her my theory about the leaking walls, and she said, "Well, I might have wet my pants." She told me she had been drinking the previous night, and thought she had been on the toilet when she peed herself, and this was the first time it had happened. We had a good laugh about it and moved on. By the time she got around to cleaning it up, it was already dry and inside the carpet.

Because she was a great roommate, I didn't think much about it until the exact same thing happened a few weeks later. It became this thing where every time Nancy drank too much, she peed in the exact same corner on the floor. I felt like I had a Chihuahua or something.

The hallway started to smell like urine, and it didn't help that the floor was carpeted. I was determined never to clean it up. I was an EMT in college and had to deal with plenty of other bodily fluids on weekends, so I did not want to deal with it in my home. We tried a few solutions. We got a cat spray that has an ammonia smell and prevents cats from peeing there, as well as a pet-stain spray to keep the smell away. There were visible stains, but thankfully we weren't the first people in the apartment to stain the carpet. I actually came close to putting a wee-wee pad there. She always put a bucket of water on the spot, but that lingering pet-spray smell never went away.

The peeing put a damper on our relationship—no pun intended. How do you have a conversation with someone about an issue like that? I encouraged her to seek medical help but I don't think she ever followed through with it. I don't know if it was my faulty communication skills, but the problem never got solved. She could still be peeing on the floor somewhere. I hear she lives alone now.

—K, 23 (F)

THE BEST FRIEND GONE WRONG

I MET STACY my freshman year, and we became fast friends. She was one of my best friends that year, so we decided to live together our sophomore year. We wanted to meet new people and roomed with two other girls we didn't know.

Stacy spent a lot of time crying over boys throughout freshman year, but I didn't think it was a big deal. When we got back to school sophomore year, Stacy had broken up with her long-distance boyfriend and was severely depressed. I thought this was a bit irrational, since she hadn't liked him all that much and was sleeping with someone else while they were in a relationship.

That first week, Stacy stayed in the room all day with the shades down, sleeping and crying. I thought maybe something else had happened that she wasn't telling me. I was concerned that she never wanted to go out or socialize. I started to make new friends because Stacy wouldn't leave the house. She only wanted to get stoned with the guy she had cheated on her ex with. She started spending more time with him, and at one point was only sleeping at our apartment once a month. There was a lot of under-the-surface tension between us.

Then in the spring, I threw a surprise birthday party for my boyfriend, who was also a good friend of hers, in our dorm. Stacy missed the surprise and showed up two hours late, stoned out of her mind with her guy, and made a big scene. I went into my bedroom as we were getting ready to leave for dinner, and she said, "Are you annoyed at me?"

"Yes, I am," I responded. "You're two hours late, which I think is disrespectful. I thought you were going to be here. So, yes, I'm annoyed at you." And she burst into tears. She was crying and heaving so hard that she couldn't catch her breath. I felt bad, but I thought she was looking for attention, and I didn't want to comfort her. Stacy locked herself in our closet, so I sent her boyfriend in to deal with it.

After we left for the restaurant, I didn't see her for the rest of the night. She didn't come back to our room for days, and when she did, we agreed that we needed to talk. Stacy was very quiet and particular about choosing her words, and said, "You hurt me. You didn't comfort me when I started crying. I was so upset over this that I've been cutting myself over the weekend. You made me feel so guilty, and this is the only way I know how to deal with it."

First of all, I felt terrible—I knew something scary was going on. Even though I didn't think I had made her cut herself, I said I was sorry and suggested that maybe she was a bit depressed and needed to see someone. During the conversation, Stacy went from talking slowly to bursting out in rage. I talked to the RAs about it afterward—I didn't think she was going to cut herself again in our apartment, but they needed to know in case it happened again.

I also had to tell our suitemates about the situation—they weren't the brightest bulbs in the world. They had both bought hamsters from Petco, and a huge cage for them. Two weeks after they got their hamsters, I went into their room and didn't see the cage. "It's in the closet," they said. "The hamsters were so loud while we were trying to sleep, and were always running on their wheels." They had no idea that hamsters were nocturnal, so they put them in the closet with a blanket over the cage. The hamsters both died, but not before one tried to eat the other one. They kept getting new hamsters (and taking care of them badly) for the rest of the year. So when I tried to explain what they needed to do if they came home and saw Stacy cutting herself, they said, "We call you, right?" "No," I said. "You call an ambulance, or somebody who can actually help her."

Thankfully, she didn't cut herself again, but I did find Prozac in our room a couple of weeks later. Even though Stacy wasn't around much, I knew she was slowly getting better, because she told me she was going to therapy. When she was there, she was super smiley and genuinely thought we were still friends. Whenever I saw her, I felt like we were walking on eggshells, and I was scared that anything I said would make her run to the bathroom.

The next year, Stacy went abroad. She messaged me a few times, and I responded once in a while, but I couldn't fake it. I was glad she wasn't my responsibility anymore, because she was in a different country. I never saw her again after that.

—C, 23 (F)

THE FAKE MOVE-OUT

I TOOK A YEAR OFF DURING COLLEGE, which I spent in upstate New York, not far from my hometown. Four of us shared a one-bedroom apartment with a living room and kitchen, with a rotating cast of roommates. The living room was big enough for us to cordon off a part of it with a tapestry to make it into another bedroom. We slept all over the apartment, including on the couch.

During the summer, we got a little crazy. We went to raves often and were always trying to have a good time. My roommate Charlotte got progressively weirder. One night we were preparing to go to a local club, and Charlotte, who had been planning on coming with us, suddenly said she was going to stay in and do some paperwork. We were all nineteen or twenty, none of us were in school, and she didn't have a job. She pulled out a folder of all these papers and started spreading them out and moving them around. It was strange, and sort of the beginning of the end.

None of us were the picture of sanity, but Charlotte was particularly eccentric and quirky. She always carried a tiny green backpack around. One night, we threw a party, and out of nowhere, she walked into the kitchen wearing her leather jacket and green backpack and started making pancakes. She didn't offer the pancakes to anyone, or say anything else, she just silently made herself breakfast in the kitchen.

She also wore glasses all the time, and one night she said to me, "People have to wear glasses because they want to see the truth." She wasn't frightening or creepy, but I always wanted to ask whether she was okay. Prior to moving in with us, Charlotte had had a heroin problem, but had gotten clean. We weren't sure if she was maybe getting high again, and never had any proof.

The other roommates and I had planned on going back to school in the fall, and wanted to get an apartment in the neighborhood where all the students lived. We started looking around, but realized that Charlotte was so unstable that we didn't want to continue to live with her or sign another yearlong lease.

Then I discovered that Charlotte had stolen a bottle of my painkillers. I used to get vicious cramps—so bad that I had to get a prescription for them. She must have thought they were muscle relaxants at first. I went to look for them one day and they weren't there. That was the incident that made me realize I had to get her out of the house.

When you're an adult, you can say, "I don't want to live with you." But we were twenty years old and thought we were so clever. A pretend move was the best idea we came up with at the time. We hatched a plan to tell Charlotte that we were all moving back in with our parents because we couldn't afford a new place.

After we told her the news, Charlotte didn't make any effort to leave or pack. We tried to ask her when she was leaving, but she didn't seem to feel any rush. So we took it to the next level. In order to sell the story, we all started packing. We bought boxes and put all our things away. I started with the most visible things, like a makeshift vanity I had. I had probably packed 75 percent of my things when she finally got her dad to pick her up. She didn't have a lot of furniture, and we somehow managed to get her to be the first person to move out. As soon as she did, we all unpacked our boxes—we decided not to move out after all—and two guy friends moved in with us.

A week later, we were at a club, and we saw Charlotte there. "Hey, I heard you guys decided to stay," she said. We made up some off-the-cuff explanation about how one of our friends decided to move in so we all stayed. We weren't prepared to see her again so soon after—it was pretty uncomfortable. I didn't stay in the apartment for much longer, because I didn't like living with guys. I never stayed in touch with Charlotte after, but she did write letters to one of our other roommates. That's how I later found out that Charlotte had moved to the West Coast with her mom, because she was being treated for schizophrenia.

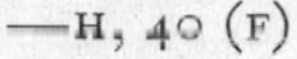
—H, 40 (F)

THE SUICIDE ATTEMPT

AFTER I TRANSFERRED COLLEGES, I met a guy, Jeremy, my junior year who I got along well with. I was a new student, so it was hard to make friends, and he was one of my first friends there. Three to four months after meeting each other, we decided to move in together. It was three of us in an off-campus apartment and we each had our own room—me, Jeremy, and another girl, Margaret.

I guess the only way to put it is that Jeremy had a lot of problems—after we moved in together, he acted very erratic. So many things that other people take in stride were devastating to him. He was happy and sad and then inconsolable for long stretches of time. He was having a lot of problems with his sort-of girlfriend, and everything was very dramatic. In retrospect, there were so many red flags at that time. I just thought Jeremy was a sensitive boy. We were all twenty-one, and this happened within a few weeks of us moving in together.

One night in September, I stayed late on campus. When I got home, I didn't notice anything was wrong, and I didn't check in with anyone. At five A.M., I got a call from Margaret, saying Jeremy was in the hospital. He had had a breakdown—that's the best way I can explain it—and flipped out. We lived in one of those old houses that had a basement, and our basement was actually an old horse stable—which was not uncommon—with wooden rafters. While I was on campus, Jeremy tried to hang himself, I think with a belt. I never saw it and I never asked. But fortunately Margaret figured out what was happening quickly, and held him up and called 911 at the same time. Jeremy was okay, but he was in a psych ward for about two weeks. His parents came out, and we had a lot of uncomfortable conversations with them and the school. The school made him take a medical leave from classes, but couldn't make him leave the apartment.

The next day, Margaret and I spent a lot of time sitting in silence and getting high. Jeremy was in the hospital and we visited him every day. It was an actual mental hospital, which neither of us were prepared for, with people talking to themselves and shouting, and a lot of people on suicide watch. We spent a week not going to class or leaving the house—instead, we drank and did cocaine at three in the afternoon. We were super numb.

After Jeremy got out of the hospital, he stayed with us for almost a month, in the same room and basically the same state. That was the worst part. I was scared all the time about what could happen. Without ever talking about it, Margaret and I took up this schedule where one of us was always home, because we were so worried. I remember feeling guilty whenever I left the house. I felt like we were the only people who knew what had happened. We didn't tell any of our friends. I only told one of my professors because I missed a bunch of class, and for a while I thought about dropping out. He convinced me not to, which I'm forever thankful for.

Jeremy was still manic and hard to reason with. I remember him flying into rages over the smallest thing. We shared groceries, which I realize now is a terrible idea to ever do with a roommate. He once sent us an all-caps e-mail about us eating too much peanut butter. It cast a weird, somber tone on all the normal roommate conflicts, and it made everything more intense.

Jeremy's parents eventually convinced him to leave. We were incredibly relieved, but the aftermath was the worst. Our washing machine was in the basement, and the rest of the time we lived in the apartment, my roommate and I only went down there together. Someone moved into his room the next semester, which made things much better. Margaret handled it well considering everything, and I was incredibly impressed by her. We both had trouble in our classes, and I had nightmares. We were so behind in our classes, we had to haul ass in order not to fail. Jeremy is now doing great, but it was the worst month of my life.

One of the things I realized after was that a lot of the classic red flags about depression or other psychological disorders apply to everyone in college. When you go to a psychiatrist, they ask, "Are you sleeping late hours? Are you sleeping a lot or a little? Are you drinking a lot?" And all of those things apply to basically all college students. So it can be hard to tell what means what. And the thing I learned most is that your home is so important, and when your home feels like a scary or hostile or uncomfortable place, it fucks your life up. I hated being home and I hated not being home. My roommate attempting suicide affected me so much more than it would have if it had just been a friend. I had to mature quickly in a short amount of time.

—E, 26 (F)

THE PLUMBING PROBLEM

AS A GRAD STUDENT, I lived in a four-person house with George and Suzie, two friends of mine from grad school. The fourth girl who was supposed to live with us backed out because she had gotten into medical school, so we found our last roommate, Molly, through Craigslist—she was an undergrad at the same school. Molly missed the deadline for university housing, and when we met her, she seemed like fun. We were a bit older than her, but felt we could all get along. Molly was not only the youngest but also the flaky girl in the house. There was a period where she stopped going to class and was staying up late but not taking responsibility for a lot of things. The rest of us weren't angels, but at least we got our stuff done.

For the most part, things went smoothly in the house. Molly was known for eating other people's ice cream, and other things that clearly weren't communal, without replacing them, but that was the sort of thing you chalked up to living with a college kid.

The basement of our apartment, which we used as storage, was unfinished and had a gutter system around the walls and the foundation. We had a bit of rain back up at some point, but nothing dramatic. We called our landlord in from time to time if there were any problems. He was a middle-aged guy who clearly didn't love us but also thought we were decent tenants because we weren't causing damage to the place and were paying rent on time.

Then in early May, as the school year was ending and all of us were taking off here and there for a couple of days or weeks at a time, we started hearing weird noises coming from the basement. It sounded like water, but when I investigated, I didn't see any problems that indicated something wasn't working properly. Then I noticed a sewagelike smell. I went back downstairs, and sure enough, the basement was flooded with sewage. George had left for the weekend, Suzie was off seeing her family, and Molly was about to fly home because her semester had ended. She hadn't been in a good place for a while, and we could tell she was on the brink of failing out of school.

I called our landlord and told him, "Our basement seems to be flooding, could you send a plumber out as soon as possible?" The plumber arrived shortly after and started mucking around downstairs. He dug out the source of the problem, which he held up to me. "I see the issue," he said. "You've got little white mice." I looked at what he was holding up and realized it was a tampon. The first thing I thought to say was, "Well, it's not mine."

"You guys can't flush these down this system," the plumber said. "This house is too old to handle this." It was a standalone 126-year-old house with original plumbing, and as far as he could tell, there were three and a half dozen tampons clogging up the system. Our basement was full of garbage disposal stuff and waste water, which had all been going into one pipe when it got stopped up.

The plumber did what he had to do, which was to unclog the pipe. "It's up to you to clean up the basement now," he said. Unfortunately, I was the only one home, and there was no way I was going to let it all sit in our basement. There's certainly no WikiHow on how to clean up a basement full of crap. So I got boots, rubber dish gloves, and a bucket and started moving all the wet cardboard boxes that we had stored in the basement. I hosed stuff down, but also picked up solid pieces of who-knows-what off the floor, because it wouldn't go back down the drain. I was fuming that I had to be the one to clean it up, because at that time, I didn't know which of the girls had done this. It could even have been George's girlfriend. And I realized, if someone was flushing tampons regularly, wouldn't it have been a problem long before now? I probably spent two to three hours fixing the gross mess and pouring bleach on the floor and scrubbing it down as much as I could. I wasn't sure what I had done to deserve this.

The next night, I got a call from our landlord and let it go to voice mail. I knew it wasn't going to be a good call. He essentially told me that he knew it wasn't my fault, but that the women in the house should have known better, and he was going to charge us for the plumber. I had to figure out how to tell the girls—I didn't want to call them up and say, what's up with your tampons clogging the plumbing?

I spoke to Suzie online briefly—we were close enough that I could ask if they were hers. "They're absolutely not mine," she said. I figured out that Molly had recently started using tampons for the first time in her life, and didn't know that you weren't supposed to flush them down the toilet. She was so preoccupied with school that it didn't occur to her that it would be an issue. In the end, we never got charged. The landlord took care of the plumbing bill, which was good, because I would have given it entirely to Molly.

Molly had been gone for three weeks or so at the time, and I had already told the story to a few people. I accidentally told one of her friends, and it somehow got back to her. When she returned, she flipped out on me. "How dare you tell that story about my personal business!" she said. As the person who had done the cleanup, I didn't think she had the right to tell me who I could and couldn't tell the story to. After all, the incident happened to me in a much different, and much grosser, way than it did to her. Molly moved out of the house shortly after.

For my next apartment, I moved across town. I found out later that my landlord gave me a great reference and said I was an absolutely wonderful tenant. It all turned out fine, but did give me a low bar for my future roommates' grossness and how much I'll put up with it.

—N, 25 (M)

THE GANG HEADQUARTERS

AS A SOPHOMORE IN OREGON, I was sick of the dorms. I'd recently been dumped by a guy, but was good friends with his sister, Carly, and she offered me a room in the cute but run-down house she was living in. I was skeptical about moving in with her, but we got along fine. Carly and I lived with a guy, Tony, who was the problematic one. He was the kind of person who never rinsed off his dishes in the sink or put the toilet seat down. When asked, he said, "My family is all guys, and we were punished for putting the toilet seat down." He was sort of incompetent—he couldn't even light a fire when we ran out of oil for the furnace while it was cold out.

In the spring, he befriended a couple of twenty-year-old girls. Looking back, I think they were a bit skanky, but I was naive and wanted to see the best in people. The three of us went away for the summer but wanted to keep our lease, so I rented my room out to Nina, a sweet, mousy lesbian girl. Carly and Tony decided to sublet to the two skanky girls, and we didn't know it at the time, but they were underage, maybe sixteen. We didn't think to check their backgrounds at all.

After we left, it only took a few weeks before the news started creeping out. The Los Angeles Crips and one of their leaders, whose nickname was Coyote, had come to town that summer and befriended the two girls. The Crips essentially made our house their headquarters. It might not have been the first drive-by shooting in our town, but it was certainly not a usual occurrence. After a couple of weeks of sharing an apartment with a gang, Nina, the girl who was staying in my room, escaped for her life.

As the summer progressed, we heard more and more about how horrible things were, between the late-night parties and the shootings in the neighborhood. The cops kept being called to our house to catch drug dealers. With help from the police, the landlords managed to evict everyone, but the house was completely trashed and everything was gone. Windows were broken and mattresses were cut up. Fashion magazines, dirty underwear, tacky clothes, fake nails, black plastic hair, and used tampons were strewn on the floor. In retrospect, I'm amazed the landlords were so nice and forgiving to us—they even bought us new box springs. We didn't have to pay for anything, though we didn't get our deposit back.

The landlords had already spent a week cleaning up when we got there, but it was still pretty bad. My down comforter was destroyed with a huge rip, Carly's bread knives, stereo, and CDs were gone, and so were my pots and pans. They sold everything they could for money and destroyed whatever was left. They even sold all my books to a used bookstore—I had to buy back books with my own name in them. There was metallic blue nail polish splashed on the dining room walls and I had to scrub them with nail polish remover. The Crips had run up huge phone bills with different companies, so we had a hard time getting our phone line back up and running.

Coyote's bills and arrest warrants kept coming to us in the fall, because he'd used our house as his address. I tried to figure what brought the Crips to our tiny town in Oregon. Our town is on the I-5 corridor, the main interstate inland along the West

Coast. I assume they were expanding their business. They weren't the smartest—Coyote and two friends left their signatures on the back of a torn map in our apartment, so it didn't take long at all for the police to find them and send them to jail.

Of course Tony, who'd brought the girls into our house in the first place, disappeared off the face of the earth. He was useless during the whole ordeal. I tried to reach him several times that year, and even called his parents, because he owed us money for the phone bills that his subletter had run up. But it was futile. In the end, his parents threatened to sue me for harassment.

—S, 43 (F)

THE GOLDFISH KILLER

MY SOPHOMORE YEAR, I lived with Mimi, a girl from my hometown. We'd gone to the same high school, but weren't really friends. We knew a lot of the same people, including Carl—he was my first kiss in middle school, and my serious crush through all of high school. He was a big figure in my life for a very long time, but I lost touch with him after graduation.

I got home one night and heard my roommate having sex. This happened fairly often, which was fine—I had sex in the room too. I stayed in the common room and let them be for a while. When they came out, there he was—my first kiss and the guy I'd crushed on forever. I didn't know he was in town. I didn't even know they'd been hanging out. I hadn't seen him in years, and they'd clearly had sex. She was wearing a bra and underwear. I never dated Carl, but Mimi knew that I had been obsessed with him from eighth grade to senior year.

Mimi had also killed my fish over spring break. It wasn't a fancy fish, it was a goldfish, and all she had to do was feed it. He died while she was taking care of him, and she told me in the form of a Facebook comment on a photo of my fish: "Tommy died. Sorry! RIP." That was her weird way of telling me. That was her style at that time. It was a very representative moment in our relationship.

Eventually, I went to bed that night, and they had sex

again—while I was there. It was a relatively big room, but it was totally obvious they were having sex. They weren't trying to be particularly quiet, and in their defense they probably thought I was asleep, but I wasn't. I'm sure if they knew I was awake they would have been a little bit more subtle. I lay there, in my shitty extra-long twin bed, and I knew if I got up and left it'd be clear I was awake the whole time. It got to the point where it'd been going on for so long I had to keep lying there. And I couldn't fall asleep—I lay there for what felt like hours but was probably more like ten minutes, because we were in college.

Once you know someone is having sex in a bed very close to you, it's the only thing you can concentrate on. It's not like I could distract myself—this was before I had a smartphone, so I couldn't text under the covers, and I couldn't read; the lights were out. There's nothing I could do except listen to sex noises and try to gauge how far they were. I remember being like, *Maybe that was it. Oh, wait. Maybe not.* You know when you're listening to classical music and it gets quiet for a little while, and you think it's over, but then it comes back even louder? It was like that.

At some point later, my roommate and I had one awful fight that ended with me throwing my French press at her—well, at the wall near her. I wasn't trying to hit her, I promise. I was just frustrated. I brought up the fact that she killed my fish, that she slept with a guy I had feelings for without telling me, and a bunch of other stuff. Honestly, it was cathartic for both of us and made our relationship better. I wasn't hurt by her sleeping with him; I was hurt by the fact that she hadn't said anything. Actually, I think I was more pissed off that she killed my fish than that she slept with this guy.

—E, 25 (F)

THE SWEDISH NEUTRALITY

I MOVED TO THE UNITED STATES from Sweden for college. I spent the first two years in South Carolina, swimming on a university team there, before I transferred to the University of Missouri. Before moving, I chatted online with my future teammate Yaniv, who was from Israel. As international students abroad, the two of us connected easily, even though Sweden and Israel are vastly different countries. It's a strange phenomenon that foreign athletes get along very easily. We knew that we were going to become great friends.

A semester later, Jowan, a friend of Yaniv's, transferred to Mizzou too. The three of us moved in together, and everyone called our house the foreigners' house. Yaniv and Jowan had been on the same swim team in Jerusalem and had known each other since they were young. What was interesting was that Yaniv was Jewish, like most Israelis, and was not overly religious but extremely patriotic. Meanwhile, Jowan was a Christian Arab. Nationality-wise, he was affiliated with Palestine and was very patriotic in that respect but also proud of his Arab roots.

It took a while for me to realize how peculiar the situation was, because back where my roommates were from, people were fighting like cats and dogs. Yaniv's mom lived in one of the settlements built by Israelis on Palestinian ground, which was a fairly vulnerable spot and where the heart of the controversy was. Their differences became tangible in late September 2011, when President Obama made a statement to the UN's general council advocating for two states, and vouched for Israel without giving much support to Palestine. That was the only time there was tension in the house. We made a conscious decision in our house not to talk about politics, but it did give me added perspective, because the two of them were on completely opposite sides of the spectrum.

A few months earlier, Jowan had become an Israeli national champion in the breaststroke, and was the first Arab to ever win a national swimming title in Israel. It was such big news that it spread to the States, particularly because it had never happened before. Jowan loved the spotlight, and I think he addressed it fairly maturely. He said that he believed the two states could live in peace, but that it's important to remember that we shouldn't turn sports into politics. I think that's the incredible thing about college swimming in the United States—it brings together people from the entire world, and they bond through sports. In swimming, there's no such thing as equipment—everyone is stripped down on the same level, and no matter what nationality you are, what language you speak, or how tall you are, none of that matters once you're in the water.

The three of us went everywhere together, from the supermarket to the bar to the gym. I asked my roommates once whether it was weird that people were fighting at home but they lived in a suite together, and they said, "Whatever happens over there doesn't affect us here," which they were proud of. Sometimes, the two of them spoke Hebrew to each other, and once in a while, they threw in an English word, like "NCAA" or "Walmart." I even picked up a bit of Hebrew, because I could gauge what they were talking about based on the situation, so I either cussed at them in Hebrew or told them to speak English.

I learned how to say "yes" and "no," and they always laughed and said I was learning.

It even became something we joked about at the bar. We often said, we're a Swede, a Jew, and an Arab living in a suite—where else are you going to find that but in Columbia, Missouri? We said that I was the neutral Swede holding down the fort, making sure that no bombs went off in the living room. It was a flawless icebreaker. I'm still in touch with both Yaniv and Jowan and sometimes spend holidays with them. I saw them a couple of weeks ago when one of our teammates got married in Iowa. Six of us came into the town, and the three Americans shared a hotel room, and Yaniv, Jowan, and I shared a room, like absolutely nothing had changed.

—A, 25 (M)

THE FAULTY WIRING

ONE NIGHT IN COLLEGE, my roommate came home drunk. She came into our bedroom and knew I kept a stash of water bottles under my desk, so she asked me for one. I gave her a bottle, which she immediately began chugging. "It's okay," I told her. "You can keep the bottle, you don't need to chug it." But she insisted on finishing it, and then went to bed.

At some point in the night, I woke up because she was fumbling around in the room. I had no idea what she was doing. I looked over and saw her squatting over her desk—which had her laptop on it—and all of a sudden, I heard the unmistakable sound of her peeing. After she finished, she stood up, changed her underwear and pants, and went straight back to bed.

Let me add that she wasn't the most hygienic person to begin with—she only washed her sheets twice a year at most, and once I saw her pull something out of her hamper and sniff it to see if she could wear it again. After she finished peeing on her desk, I asked if she needed any help cleaning up. She said, "No, why?" and fell back asleep. I tried to doze off as well, but all I could hear was *bzzzzt. Drip. Drip. Bzzzzt. Drip. Drip*—the sound of her laptop short-circuiting.

The next morning, she woke up and asked me if our electricity was out. "My computer isn't turning on," she said. And I had to tell her that she peed on it last night, but she didn't believe me! So I asked, "Is your computer wet?" She said it was and asked me if it had rained last night. I could only reply with "No, that's your pee."

When I came home later that afternoon, she was drying her laptop with a blow-dryer. She later took it to a computer lab to get it looked at. I feel really bad for the lab technician who had to deal with that.

—L, 27 (F)

THE PRINCESS PALACE DREAM

THE FIRST TIME I MOVED AWAY FROM HOME, I decided to move in with my best friend, Lila. We were super excited about getting an apartment together, and finally found a three-bedroom basement apartment. We needed a third person to fill the last bedroom, and Lila had a friend, Olivia, who volunteered to take the room. We thought this was going to be the perfect scenario, because it meant we could avoid going on Craigslist or Gumtree (a classifieds site in the UK) or any of those routes to get a housemate.

At this point in our lives, we weren't jaded yet, we'd never had roommates before, and we were so excited about moving away from home into an apartment and painting the living room a bright neon pink and eating pizza every day. At that time, we thought the apartment was amazing, but I recently went back to visit, and it was the scuzziest place you can imagine. It had bars on all the windows, and it was tiny, damp, and on a horrible block. But because it was ours, we were so proud of it.

After we moved in, everything was great for about a week. Olivia was nice, but she kept to herself a lot. I put that down to the fact that she moved in with two best friends who were very close, so maybe she felt a bit left out. But in week two, she came out dressed to go on a date—and she had my top on. I was a bit taken aback that she had brazenly walked out wearing something that I knew was mine. It was a recognizable piece, certainly not a standard top from Topshop. I was so shocked that I didn't say anything until she came home. When she did, I asked her, "Did you borrow my top? It's fine, but it would have been nice to know in advance."

"No," she said. "This is my top, I've had it for two years. My mom bought it for me." And she waltzed back into her room. This became a recurring pattern. When we weren't in, she went into our rooms and took things she liked. If we called her out on it, she claimed they were her own. There's not much you can do when someone says that, because other than stitching a name label on your clothes, how else can you prove it's yours? Olivia had a great time enhancing her wardrobe while we lost most of our favorite things. She never returned the items, and we were so keen on this dream of living together that we didn't want to cause any friction or arguments.

In the two months we lived together, I think she took at least twenty pieces of clothing from us. She had the most intricate stories, like, "Oh, my friend was in Japan and she bought this for me." She would be really offended if we dared to suggest it was ours.

That was the first warning sign, but we kind of let it go. We lived in such a shady old apartment that when you were in the shower, if anyone turned on the sink in the kitchen, the shower would go freezing cold. I noticed that every time I took a shower, the heat went on and off. It was almost a joke how bad it was. One time, I left the shower running and crept down the hallway. Olivia was in the kitchen turning the tap on, off, on, off. She wasn't using the sink or doing the dishes, she was just torturing me while I was in the shower. It was bizarre behavior. It was hard to bring these things up with her because she never seemed guilty or embarrassed. She didn't seem to think she was doing anything wrong. One time I came home and thought no one was in because the whole apartment was pitch-black. I turned on the hallway light, and Olivia's bedroom door was open and she was lying on her bed staring at the ceiling. It was about a month of this until we started to get freaked out.

While we were living there, we noticed that we were going through toilet paper ridiculously quickly. At some point, each of us bought our own toilet paper, because it was such a contentious issue of who was buying it and why it was never stocked up. We went through so many rolls a week—none of us could work out how on earth we could be using so much toilet paper. One day, I was cleaning up and Olivia was out, so I decided to go to her room to collect a few glasses. There was a mug on the floor, and I bent down to pick it up. Under the bed, there must have been a hundred rolls of toilet paper, all different sizes, some nearly used down, some entire rolls. She'd taken them to either torment us or to make us buy more. No one could ever need that much toilet paper.

Things came to a head two months in. At the time, Lila was working in a record store. One day, this unsavory-looking girl, who didn't quite look like someone we'd hang out with, walked up to her, and said, "Hi, I'm Christy, and I'm taking Olivia's room." She saw the room advertised on Gumtree, had looked at our apartment, had the keys, and said she was moving in that week. This was the first we'd heard of it. Olivia hadn't told us that she was moving out of her room or that she'd showed it and chosen someone.

Obviously, this didn't go down well at all with us. This was a Friday, and Christy was due to move in on Monday. The landlord agreed that if we could find a new replacement by Monday, we could choose who moved in. Lila's boyfriend was the only person we could trust to move in with two days' notice. They had only been together for six months, but it was either him or a psycho.

When Olivia moved out, we didn't want to be in her way—things ended badly, she didn't enjoy living with us, and we certainly didn't enjoyed living with her. The next day, we scouted around and realized she'd stolen random things from the apartment that belonged to us, like a couple of packets of hot chocolate, a packet of needles, a pizza that was in the freezer, and a toothbrush. It was like she was preparing to go to war or something. It felt like she was taking small, strange objects to remind her of the time in the apartment, the way a serial killer takes souvenirs.

Once Olivia left, Lila's boyfriend moved in, and that was a whole other nightmare, because then I was living with a couple. My best friend and I had moved in together thinking we were going to live in a princess palace, with pink everything, and watch *Powerpuff Girls* and have cocktail hour. It was a girly dream. Her boyfriend wasn't a bad guy, but as soon as I was living with a couple, it was a completely different dynamic. Whenever we wanted to go out, he always had to come.

Once, we planned a huge night out, and even bought tickets to a club in advance. I was single and wanted to go out and meet people. That night, we had been drinking in the apartment and getting ready, and were completely dressed and at the door. All of a sudden, her boyfriend said, "I don't want to go. My legs hurt." It was the most random excuse ever. Lila asked if we could still go, and he said, "No, can you stay home and look after me?" Then I obviously couldn't go either, and we all sat at home, dressed up, in silence. It went from bad to worse, but at least he didn't hoard toilet paper or torture me in the shower like Olivia had. It was so awkward whenever the two of us were the only ones in the apartment; we even avoided being in the kitchen at the same time.

After the year was up, I was so traumatized that I moved back home—luckily, I could still commute to the university. And that living room we painted neon pink? On moving-out day, Lila's parents had to repaint the whole room back to magnolia. It was such a bright paint that it took them five coats to cover it. They were not happy about that. Lila and I are still best friends, but we never lived together again. The princess palace dream went away.

—B, 29 (F)

THE RECOVERED ADDICT

WHILE FINISHING MY DOCTORATE, I lived in a three-bedroom house with Chad, a buddy from work who I thought was a recovered alcoholic. He was six years older than me, and I'm not sure why he agreed to move in—maybe to help me with bills, or because he thought it would be good for him to live with someone else. It wasn't until I found out he was still drinking that all sorts of weird things started to make sense.

I woke up one day and he had broken the kitchen table and the window right next to it. He claimed he had come home in the dark and tripped. Granted, the table was cheap, with one of those pressboard tops, so the screws underneath were not great. It had come off its base, and I assumed he had put his elbow through the glass window. But the idea of tripping in the dark was a bit unbelievable—it makes more sense that he was stumbling around drunk.

Chad was constantly washing all his comforters. He always went to bed with a huge pitcher of water because he got really thirsty, and he claimed that he spilled the pitcher of water on himself at night. He was clearly wetting the bed, and this happened almost once a month.

I also think he was peeing out his bedroom window at night. I thought I was going crazy, because our bedrooms were on the second floor next to each other, facing the front of the house. I often heard the window open while I was sleeping, and could hear what sounded like peeing on the shingles. At the time I thought, *Is he so lazy that he can't even go to the bathroom to pour out his pitcher of water?* That's how blind I was to the whole thing. I didn't want to get up out of my bed and look because I didn't want to know the answer.

I never saw Chad drink, but I knew he had a past with alcohol. One time, friends of mine from Germany were staying with us and had brought me a bottle of liqueur. We went out overnight, and when we came back, we couldn't find the bottle. I asked Chad if he'd moved it, but I was so convinced he was recovered that I believed him when he said he knew nothing about it.

One Saturday morning, I was lying in bed upstairs when I heard my neighbor downstairs yelling, "Hello? Anyone here?" I came running down, and she said, "Your buddy's on the front porch. I think he fell off the porch swing." I ran out and saw Chad, almost catatonic, rocking back and forth on the floor. He'd fallen off the swing and his eyes were dilated and glassy. He was so nonresponsive that I called 911, but by the time they arrived he was back in his bedroom. The police went up to his room, which was closed, and asked me if there was any chance he was dangerous. "No," I said. "He's a ninety-pound weakling."

They went into his room, which I hadn't been in for months. I kept saying, "He's on antidepressants, he sees a psychologist." And they said, "No, ma'am, he's drunk." I told them he didn't drink anymore, but they looked under the bed, and it was filled with bottles in brown paper bags. I felt like a complete idiot and couldn't believe I was so willfully blind to the fact that he was a functioning alcoholic.

I was so furious I wanted Chad committed. He's a cigarette smoker, and I was afraid he would burn down my house while

I was out. The police couldn't have him committed, but they helped me get him into my car so I could take him to the hospital. On the way there, I kept yelling at him to give me his family's home phone number so I could have someone come get him. This was also the day I was supposed to send in my dissertation proposal, which I had to postpone. I went through Chad's wallet to get his sister's phone number. But it was a Saturday, and she had married an Orthodox Jewish man, so she wasn't answering the phone that day. I called the police in his sister's town, and asked them to knock on her door and have her check her machine. I told her I wanted to have Chad committed, but she's a doctor and told me that he couldn't be committed against his will. She contacted other family they had in Ohio, who were a few hours away, to come deal with him. But he kept denying he had a problem, and said I was overreacting. After that ordeal, I kicked him out of the house. While we were living together, I didn't even realize what a crappy situation it was—I guess I thought that was life.

Unfortunately, a couple of years later, after I had moved away, somebody called me to let me know that Chad had been found dead in his apartment. He had been fired from the public radio station where I met him. Since he was unemployed, no one was aware that he wasn't checking in to work. The landlord noticed the mail piling up, and that's how they found him. He was only in his thirties, and drank himself to death.

—J, 45 (F)

THE MULTIPLE PERSONALITIES

DURING COLLEGE IN THE MIDWEST, I signed up for an off-campus apartment complex and was placed with five other girls. Most of us were students in our early twenties, except Sandra, who was a bit older.

All six of us went to church together and slowly got to know one another. It wasn't until after the summer that we learned about Sandra's dissociative identity disorder. When she moved in, Sandra had hoped that we wouldn't have to know, but she realized she couldn't function in a situation with five strangers not knowing about her condition. She told us she had been abused when she was younger and often had regressions. Depending on the trigger, she might scream or freak out, as if the abuse were happening to her again.

She had been in heavy therapy—in fact, before she came to live with us, she was living in a mental health facility. She was trying to get better, and had moved into our college town to be closer to a therapist who was working with her. None of us had any idea we'd be exposed to this, but we dealt with it pretty well. Opening up about it helped her heal. We were all religious and wanted to do what we could to help her out. Sandra didn't have much family as a support system—her mom had passed away and she had an elderly father who wasn't able to take care of her and an older sister who was paralyzed from the waist down.

After a particularly violent episode, where one of her personalities smashed all our mugs in the sink and was cutting her hands on the shards, Sandra suggested that we go to roommate therapy—the same way you go to family therapy when someone has a mental health issue.

We all went to meet with the therapist, together and separately, who gave us methods for coping and for understanding what Sandra was going through. We learned a lot about her history. When she was abused, her personality was split so Sandra, the core person, didn't have to deal mentally with the abuse. Through therapy, she was trying to integrate those multiple personalities into her core being so she could accept what had happened to her.

In the two years we lived together, I probably met five or six of her personalities. I remember Blue Eyes, Johnny, the Hero, the Nightmare, and the Playgirl. Once, I was talking to Sandra, the core personality, and she froze. As I watched, her hazel eyes turned bright blue. It was the weirdest thing I've ever experienced. I don't know how it was physically possible. Blue Eyes also blinked and didn't speak. Some of the others, like Johnny, did.

Johnny was a thirteen-year-old boy who was very funny. We interacted with him the most. It's weird to say, but he was a cute kid who came out when we were playing. Once, he wanted to shave Sandra's eyebrows, though we didn't think she'd like that. The Nightmare was the one who broke the mugs—she was scary violent. I actually took a knife away from her once, and got a cut on my hand. I still have a scar from that. There was another personality I only met once who called himself the Hero. He was young, and he said he protected Sandra from bad men. That broke my heart. And the Playgirl didn't interact with us much, but had a very promiscuous personality.

When she came out of the regressions, she didn't usually remember what had happened. She only recognized that she was waking up and things were different. She described it once as, "You're at the top of the stairs and hear things that are going on, but you don't know what's happening downstairs." We only told her what had happened if she asked, because we didn't want to make her feel guilty.

The therapist told us there was nothing we could do when a personality came out. The best thing to do, he said, was to continue to act normally, since we couldn't avoid them. The only thing we could do was make sure we didn't get hurt. He believed Sandra was strong enough that she would stop herself if one of the personalities put her in danger. Sometimes, if it was a milder personality, we'd say things like, "Can Sandra come out? We need to go to church." The therapist gave us many tips to deal with it, and we had his number if we ever needed to call him.

Not all the personalities were aware of one another, and Sandra wasn't aware of all of them. It depended on how far she was in her integration. The milder personalities stemmed from less severe abuse, whereas the therapist told us the more intense personalities came from ritualistic abuse. Johnny seemed to be the most aware of them all, and in the two years we lived together, she was able to integrate him. Sandra was able to recognize the abuse he had come from and own that it had happened to her, and that's when he ceased to exist. But as she integrated the easier ones, the others became a lot harsher. So she was improving from a therapeutic standpoint, but living with her became harder.

We never knew what would trigger her. Church was hard, because she'd been abused by a church leader, so we were all on alert when we were there. Surprises also triggered her, so we learned to announce ourselves before touching her or getting her attention. As she progressed, she started to realize if she was getting uncomfortable—such as if we were watching a movie that was dark—and she knew to remove herself from the situation. She took responsibility for herself in that way. At the core, she was a very talented and sweet girl.

Once, all of the roommates went on a vacation to California together. Sandra was normal the whole trip and it was so much fun. There were hard times, but we had good memories too. The girl who roomed with Sandra was an inherent caregiver, and had been planning to study math, but instead went into the health profession as a nurse. I think living with Sandra defined her life—she realized how much she could affect someone who needed help.

I moved out of the apartment to live abroad for eighteen months. Partway through my trip, Sandra's personalities got so violent that they had to put her in another home. She's living on her own now and doing well. When I look back on it, it wasn't a traumatizing experience—the roommate therapy truly helped. We were in it together, and it forced us to bond and support one another. The six of us lived together for more than two years, and I'm undoubtedly closer to them than any other group of roommates I ever had.

—R, 35 (F)

ADVENTURES ABROAD

THE KLEPTOMANIAC

I SPENT MY FRESHMAN YEAR of college in Florence. Most rooms in our dorm had three or four people living in them, but we had a huge corner room with five girls total. It had high ceilings and was a relatively large space—we even had a private bathroom, while everyone else on the floor had to share a communal one. It was set up as two bunk beds and a single, which I had for the first semester. My roommates were from all over the world—Malaysia, Germany, Qatar, China. We were all different in personality, but when you live in such close quarters, you have to get along. Maybe it was a six-month honeymoon stage, but we were strangely close. We traveled a lot together, and even spent Thanksgiving in Qatar at Lana's house. When I came back from winter break, I remember being happy to see them again.

During the second semester, things started going missing in the dorm. One girl in our building lost an expensive fur coat. Two of my roommates bought international calling cards in bulk, and a few of them went missing at a time, but we didn't think much of it because they were only about fifteen euros. Then one morning, I woke up and for some reason thought, *I have to check the drawer under my bed*. It was the only lockable compartment we had, but it wasn't secure at all. We were close enough that

I didn't lock my drawer anyway. I had six hundred euros stashed there under my clothes, and when I checked, five hundred of it was missing, as well as a bit of currency from my home country that I'd put there for nostalgia's sake. There was so much missing that I was in disbelief. I remember opening and closing the drawer, and wondering, *Did that happen? Am I dreaming?* My roommates felt terrible for me and offered to spot me money. The RAs weren't very helpful, and it was something I had to let go.

Soon after, another roommate, Cathy from Malaysia, had three hundred euros go missing, and Lana told us that she had four hundred euros go missing, as well as a diamond ring her grandmother had given her. That's when things blew up and we realized it wasn't an isolated case anymore. Even then, we were sort of still in denial that it could be one of us because we were such good friends. But at the same time, there were five of us in the room. It's unlikely that someone could have come in while we were all out. By this point it began to dawn on us that the culprit had to be someone in the room because there was almost always one of us in the room at any given time. It wasn't until later, when another roommate, Tina from China, left her wallet on her desk while she was in the shower and two hundred euros went missing, that the accusations started flying. The only person awake at that time was Julie, whose desk was next to hers, and Tina immediately assumed she was the thief. She spoke to Lana and me, and Lana became very defensive. "This doesn't feel right, I don't want to accuse Julie," she said. I thought the facts were suspicious, but knew it was something we needed to talk about. Tina and I spoke to Julie, who was typically very shy and reserved, and she was visibly super upset. We didn't have any proof and couldn't draw a conclusion, so we brought it back to the room for a larger discussion. We were all pointing fingers at one another and claiming it wasn't us, since we had all had money stolen from us. Suddenly, everyone was a potential enemy.

It was very battle royal—anyone could turn on you at any moment.

During the argument, Tina and Lana clashed the most, with Lana claiming that it wasn't fair for Tina to turn on Julie and accuse her. Lana even went to the RAs and said that Tina and I were going around accusing people of stealing money left and right. It was a standstill where we couldn't get any help and we had to continue living with one another in a single room, so the next few months were miserable. Lana and Julie became closer, and Lana turned the campus against Tina and Cathy, which broke our room apart. And Tina was unhappy with me because the two sides hated each other but I was trying to be neutral. It was such a dark transition from the previous semester, when we traveled together and hung out all the time.

After the big talk, for a while nothing went missing. Tina was now convinced that Lana was the thief, but we no longer bothered pointing fingers. Much later in the semester, I was in the dorm's study room, and Lana said to me, "I'm going to go to our friend Vic's room for a smoke." Ten minutes later, Lana came back and abruptly announced she'd lost four hundred euros. Then a few hours later, Vic's roommate came by and told me that Vic was missing a hundred euros. The roommate had returned to their room earlier and Lana was the only one there, and looked shocked to see him. That's when he said to me, "I'm starting to believe she did steal money from you guys." At this point, the whole campus knew about it. There were only about a hundred of us in Florence, so word spread quickly.

In our last week in Florence, right before Tina was about to take a trip to London, she lost ninety pounds. The night before, she and Lana had gotten into a disagreement of sorts—Tina found out Lana had used her computer to send herself a bunch of movies, and since they were deep enemies at this point, she was infuriated that Lana used her computer without asking. Tina woke me up early that morning to tell me her money went missing, which she needed because she was about to go to London. So she went to Lana, and in a gentle way said, "Hey, did you take my money? I don't care if you did, but I need that money." Lana denied it completely. It was a painful morning, and I don't even know how Tina's money was taken—she slept on an upper bunk with her wallet next to her head.

We all parted ways at the end of the semester, and after I got home, I received a call from Julie, the girl we had first accused of being the thief and Lana's only friend in the room. Since Julie was from Germany, she was the only one with an ATM card while abroad. Her parents had looked at all of the transactions on her card, and noticed that there were a bunch of withdrawals at three or four in the morning, totaling up to a thousand euros. The only person in our room who stayed up that late was Lana. The card had a PIN, but they often went to the ATM together. And Julie thought the two of them were such good friends because Lana had to come to her defense, and boom, there goes a thousand euros. The worst part was, they were planning on rooming together the following year.

We never got a confession out of Lana, but at this point we all knew it was her. She had a tendency to not be truthful in general. While in Florence, she flew home at least once a month to visit her boyfriend. She told us that her family was funding these trips because they were wealthy, but when we visited them in Qatar over Thanksgiving, we found out her parents didn't know she was coming back—they didn't approve of her boyfriend and certainly weren't paying for the flights. The only way she could have afforded those flights was probably from the money she took from us. She was also a crazy girlfriend—there were nights where she screamed at her boyfriend over the phone at the top of her lungs at two A.M.

The incident that sealed the deal for me was during our junior year back in the States, almost two years later, when Lana and I met up because we were taking the same class and decided to study together. We had maintained a friendly facade after the mess of our first year, and I wanted to put those events behind me. But as she greeted me and we sat down together for the first time in years, the one thing I noticed was the very distinctive diamond ring on her finger—the exact gift from her grandmother she had claimed was stolen.

—J, 28 (F)

THE FOREIGN EXCHANGE STUDENT

I'VE ALWAYS HAD a very strong interest in Africa, and I thought Botswana would be a cool, off-the-beaten-path place to study abroad. It appealed to me because not many people went there—I was actually the first from my college to study abroad there.

I arrived at the University of Botswana with no idea what I was getting myself into. Nothing was what I'd expected it to be, which goes to show how little we truly know about what we're going to encounter in a foreign country before we show up there. For the most well-rounded experience possible, the program paired Americans with local Setswanan-speaking students as roommates. And for half the time we were there, we had to do a homestay in a nearby village, which required us to hitchhike to school in the morning and back because there was no bus. We often stood out on the road, hoping that there was someone making the half-hour drive to our university.

Our dorm, which was relatively new and sparse-looking, resembled a military compound or prison cell. Then we realized that there was no air-conditioning or hot water. We arrived at the tail end of winter, and since Botswana is sort of desertlike, it gets hot during the day and cold at night. We sweated during the days, with no hot water to shower with. This being Africa, there was a Chinese construction firm building a stadium down the road from us. Rather than laying more pipes for water, they diverted all the hot water to the construction site. Midway through the semester, all the water had been diverted, so if you wanted to brush your teeth in the morning, you had to go outside and find a spigot or sprinkler.

My roommate, Keletso, was absolutely gorgeous but really shy. She didn't speak to me for the first two weeks, so I thought she hated me. But it turned out that it was because her English wasn't that great. I also thought she didn't know my name, because she kept calling me "Lekgowa." It took me about two weeks to realize that *lekgowa* is the generic term for white person. That's what she called me all semester. I was the first white person Keletso had ever met. All her friends came over, and they took turns hanging out with her and sitting on her bed and staring at me across the room. Sometimes they took out their camera phones and pretended to be texting but were really taking photos of me. It was hilarious. I always told them it was okay, but they never came over to my side of the room. If I talked to them, they giggled and ran away or asked me questions like, "How rich is everybody in America?" There was one guy who every single time I met him said, "How much money do you have?" It was one of those culture shock moments—in his mind, every single person who is a white Westerner is extremely wealthy.

Every morning, I was woken up at four thirty A.M. by my floormates' shower ritual. Everyone had her own kettle to boil water in, because there was no hot water in the dorm. In order to avoid a cold shower, the girls made multiple trips—while wearing nothing but a shower cap—from the bathroom and back to heat up enough water for a small bathtub's worth of water. Everyone made fun of me for refusing to take off my towel. Throughout the process, you could hear music blasting from the rooms—a mixture of American pop music from nine months ago—that's how long it took for music to get to Botswana—and Setswanan gospel music.

After the multiple trips to get water, Keletso stood in the middle of our room, which had linoleum tile floors, and started scooping cups of water over her body to take a bath. And she always worried about me getting sick because I took cold showers. I'd rather shiver in the freezing cold than go through all that for a hot shower every morning. I did try it once, because I wanted a hot shower and I thought maybe it wouldn't be so bad. But it was too much work for one shower.

There were bathrooms on each floor of the dorm, with two showers, two sinks, and two toilets, but they were always packed. It was all about the hierarchy—only the two oldest girls on each floor were able to use the showers. There was none of that whole "I have class, do you mind if I dash in before you?" thing. The eldest girls took as long as they wanted and no one questioned them. And there was no running water, so if you wanted to use the toilet, you had to go outside and bring in water to pour down the toilet to get it to work.

It all brought up this bigger question of water in Botswana, which Keletso taught me about. *Pula* is the Setswanan word for currency, blood, and water, and it's the word they shout in celebrations. They never waste water there. One of the best moments I had with her was when we were sitting in the dorm one very hot night. I'd been there for almost three months, and it hadn't rained at all. All of a sudden, you could smell a difference in the air, like rain was coming. Keletso sat up and said, "Come with me." As we were running downstairs, it started to rain, and everyone in the surrounding dorms sprinted outside and was all chanting "*pula*" and doing this cool dance. "Do you get it now?" said Keletso. I don't know if I'll ever truly get it, but I understood where she was coming from after that. Living in a permanent drought culture will make you appreciate water and showers.

Every two weeks, Keletso got these elaborate weaves and hairstyles done. But before she could go to the salon, she had to take the existing braids out first. She always sat on my bed with a brush and waited for me to stop whatever I was doing to help her unbraid the hundreds of braids in her head. It took about three hours, and I realized that I had absolutely no idea of the amount of work that goes into an African's hair. Most of the girls did it together, and we joked that you always knew when it was Sunday hair day by looking out the window. There were always tumbleweeds of discarded fake black hair after everybody spent the whole day taking it out. These three hours of unbraiding hair were the only time we truly talked. Keletso was so quiet most of the time that it was hard to get her to open up. She was a quiet person, and anything she said was usually to help me understand what I thought of as the absurd parts of life there.

For instance, in Botswana, there are these locustlike giant flying ants, almost like cicadas, which come out every seven years. No one told us to expect this at all, and one day, we heard a low hum, and a black cloud came toward us. All of a sudden, we saw an enormous swarm of flying ants. It was so bizarre, it felt like we were in an apocalypse. I didn't know what to do, what they were, or whether they would sting. We study-abroad kids were screaming and running to our rooms—it felt like a blizzard of bugs. I got to my room and started slamming the doors shut, stuffing towels in the cracks and closing windows. Meanwhile, Keletso was as calm as can be. She walked around the room with a little basket, picking the bugs up and tearing off their wings, popping a few into her mouth live and putting others in a basket to eat later. It was my worst nightmare, and she was telling me how tasty the bugs were. She thought I was absolutely insane not to want to eat them. For her, food was literally falling from the sky.

When we finally left the room, the door was sticking because there was actually a mound of bugs against the other side. Sweepers had to come in and go through the hallways to clear a path. The bugs lasted for twenty-four hours and then suddenly died. I did try one eventually, after they fried it and I knew it was thoroughly dead. It wasn't as bad as I thought it would be—I pretended it was a Cheeto. I'm an adventurous eater, but I had to pass on the living bugs.

Later in the semester, when my homestay fell through for a variety of reasons, Keletso told me to stay with her family. She had lots of younger siblings, and her family was incredibly generous and hospitable. Since my family's Italian, I wanted to cook a traditional Italian meal for them to thank them for hosting me. I got all the ingredients for spaghetti and meatballs, and it took me hours to make a huge pot of it because the power kept going out. We all sat down for dinner; they'd never had pasta before—they kept calling it macaroni, since they were familiar with Kraft macaroni and cheese packets. I was nervous about them liking the food. I gave them huge portions, and they all sat there, quietly eating. All of a sudden, the youngest brother started to cry. He didn't speak any English, so he said something in Setswana to his mom, and she started laughing. It turned out he wasn't crying because he didn't like it but because he wanted to eat it all and didn't have any more room in his stomach. "It's okay," his mom said. "We have a solution." And they all stood up from the table after having eaten this heavy pasta meal and, with totally straight faces, put their hands in the air and started jogging through the house to settle the food. After ten minutes of this running around with their hands in the air, roller-coaster-style, they sat back down and ate another full portion of the pasta. I had made enough for at least twelve people, and the five of us finished it all. I guess it was a huge compliment. At the end of the homestay, they asked me to take a photo with them. It started with the immediate family, but then they said, "Wait, we need to get our goat in the picture." Then the neighbors also wanted a photo, and extended family came by to drop things off and also wanted one. The next thing I knew, it was a two-and-a-half-hour process. The majority of them had never met an American before and thought it was a novelty.

I loved living with Keletso. She's a phenomenal runner and hopefully will represent Botswana in the Olympics someday. Living in Botswana was an incredibly life-changing experience. Every single thing you take for granted in your life, from amenities to ways of communicating, was so fundamentally different. I wouldn't have been able to process what I was going through without her quiet guidance.

—R, 25 (F)

THE MANIC-DEPRESSIVE

WHEN I MOVED TO FRANCE for my postdoctoral program, I didn't know anyone else who was going to be there. I met Brad through a friend, who told me that he was another American who was going to be at the same institute as me. The two of us exchanged a few brief e-mails and agreed to split a place to save money. It sounded better to have a friend of a friend than nobody at all. I got there four or five weeks before he did and did a lot of the legwork of finding an apartment for us.

We got along fine when we met. I could tell Brad had been through a few weird things in life. He'd taken a year off from grad school and had basically gotten stoned the entire time—he was a wacky guy and crazy things happened to him one way or another. In our first few weeks living together, I noticed that he constantly got stoned or drunk, went on shopping binges, or spent days watching television. It was as if he had poor impulse control. He was thirty-two, but was still immature and had a lot to figure out.

Then in the spring, Brad told me he was taking himself off his depression medication, because he felt fine. I didn't even know that he was taking anything, but assumed he was dealing with it in a somewhat responsible manner. A couple of weeks went by, and that's when things began to get really frustrating.

Brad started staying up later and later, drinking more heavily, and stopped caring about his job or being healthy. By June, he was staying out at the bars until two A.M. on weeknights and inviting a dozen strangers over to play music in our living room at three in the morning. This happened several nights in a row, until I sat him down and said, "I'm not trying to cut into your social life, but I live here." He always apologized and said he'd be better in the future, or offered to make me dinner to make up for it. But the cycle kept happening over and over again.

One afternoon I came home and discovered that he'd gone on an afternoon shopping spree and purchased two guitars and motorcycle clothing. His on-again, off-again girlfriend, Lisa, was concerned that he was buying much more than normal. She had sat him down to try to get him help because he was off his meds, but he refused. An older friend of Brad's, Gary, who's in his early fifties but has lived a rock-and-roll lifestyle, called to ask how Brad was doing. "Keep an eye on him," he said. "I'm concerned about him."

Brad had also started hanging out with the homeless guys in the neighborhood, who he met at the shelter a block or so away. He bummed around with them in the afternoons and evenings and bought them a couple of beers. He wasn't an extrovert, let alone someone who cared about the plight of the homeless. But he found them interesting, and stood around and chatted with them. He was surprised that once he started hanging out with homeless people, others thought he was homeless as well.

One evening, I got home late after dinner with friends to find that our apartment was completely filled with junk Brad had purchased from a secondhand store in the neighborhood—everything from ironing boards to an electric lawnmower to tool sets and clothes. It was easily a thousand euros of crap. That's when it hit me how bad it was. I saw him on the balcony drinking beers with a homeless guy, and he asked if I wanted to meet his friend, a known crack addict. Instead, I went upstairs, grabbed my laptop, passport, a few changes of clothing, and called Lisa, who by then was his ex. "Things have gotten bad," I said. "Come over now." We called emergency mental health services, but they told us that they couldn't help him unless he was in imminent danger to himself or others or volunteered to be committed.

We agreed that we'd try to talk to Brad together, but when we got home, he wasn't there. We searched the town to try to find him and stage some type of three A.M. intervention. When we next saw him days later, I told him we had to talk. "Everything's fine," he said. "I'm a little depressed but trying to feel better." He didn't realize how bad it'd gotten for the rest of us. He agreed to move out, and his dad happened to be coming into town the next day.

When his dad arrived, he knew there was a crisis going on—he had seen all the symptoms of an oncoming manic phase from eight thousand miles away. It was nine in the morning and Brad was chugging a bottle of gin while chain-smoking and pounding cups of coffee. He made his dad take him to a prostitute. He had a ton of sexual energy and needed to blow off steam somehow. He even proposed that the two of us get a prostitute housekeeper to straighten up so we didn't have to do too much cleaning, and that we could share her. That was without a doubt one of the craziest things I've ever heard come out of another person's mouth.

His dad told me that Brad had been diagnosed with bipolar disorder awhile back, and that it ran in the family. He clearly needed to be back on his meds as soon as possible, and in the meantime, they were hoping he would wear himself out. I left town for the weekend, because I needed to walk away.

When I got back, Brad had invited one of the crack addicts to stay in our living room. "I hope that's okay with you," he said, though it absolutely wasn't. By the end of that week, Gary and Brad's father managed to sit him down and tell him he needed help. They got him to go to the emergency room, where he got medication and finally managed to get himself to sleep—a small miracle in itself. I left the country again for another vacation, and honestly didn't know if I'd see my home ever again. Brad sent me a long text message, rambling about how I needed to move out because I was the one with the problem, not him.

Brad finally got treatment and left his job, which wasn't stable to begin with. Around the time he got medicated, he met a girl standing in line at the bank. They supposedly fell in love—she seemed like a clueless naive girl and he was a person in a manic phase who couldn't tell love from being hyper. The two of them moved to San Francisco—it didn't hurt that she was having visa issues and had to leave the country sooner rather than later. His dad, who was still sleeping on our couch, had to clean up the whole apartment, and did an amazing job of getting rid of the stuff from the secondhand store. When Brad left, he told me he hoped we could still be friends. "We'll see," I said. He was taking his meds, but still in rough shape. Two months later, he proposed to the girl he met at the bank.

I haven't heard from Brad in a few years now, with one exception. When we were living together, we set up automated rent payments so his account automatically sent me five hundred euros a month and I paid the landlord. He e-mailed me from San Francisco to ask if I'd forgotten to turn off the payment system. I told him that I had settled things with the landlord, but he was the one who had to stop his account from sending me the money every month. He moved out in August 2011, and I'm still getting rent payments from him. I've tried to have my bank stop the payments, but they said they couldn't do anything about it without him canceling the payments—and I don't know if he ever will. Every time I get five hundred euros from him, I send it back to an account that he probably never checks. I'd feel way too dirty keeping the money.

—N, 29 (M)

THE BUSINESS SHOWER

I STUDIED ABROAD in Eastern Europe, and as a European history major, I was one of the few people who was actually abroad for a reason other than drinking beer. All the study abroad students lived in an apartment building in a swanky suburb, like an island of Americans. I spent two semesters there, and during the first, I lived in a triple. In my second semester, I moved into the single bedroom in our suite, and my three new roommates were a weird bunch. There was Tom, a budding politician who had run for city council in his hometown. He had a big personality and got into philosophical fights with everyone. Then there was an artist named Mitch, who rarely wore pants in the dorms—just long T-shirts and Timberland boots. He also carried around bread in a grocery bag to bars and restaurants because he wanted to save money. And finally, Joe, a preppy frat guy who seemed dumbfounded by the whole experience. We got along well considering how different we were.

Every morning, we all had class at the same time, and there was always a bathroom traffic jam. On more than one occasion, I opened the door to find one of the people from the triple walking out at the same time. I always said, "Whoever needs to get to class or their internship earlier should feel free to go ahead," but Tom's response, more than once, was, "Let's take a business shower."

This was a weird, awkward thing I'd never heard of before, so I said, "What are you talking about?" And Tom said, "It's where two roommates take a shower together because they have to get to work or class on time. It's a totally normal thing." I laughed it off, because Tom was so goofy. He was openly gay, but I don't think it was ever meant to be a come-on. It was simply his awkwardness.

A year later, I got back from abroad and saw on some blog that the slang word of the day was "business shower." I clicked on the link, and the definition went something like this: "An intimate shower taken between two persons solely for the purpose of saving time, completely devoid of any sexual connotation." There was a sample conversation where two people were talking, and one suggested showering together, to which the response was, "Hey man, that's gross." Then the first guy explained it would be a business shower, and the second said, "Aight, dog." I looked for the author, and it was a username that was similar to one Tom used. I don't think I've ever said, "Hey man, that's gross" or "Aight, dog" in my life.

I don't know if Tom ever told any of our other roommates about the business shower, or whether he heard it from someone else and maybe became the person to write down an official definition online. I never took him up on the business shower, though I'm curious to know what would have happened. Has anyone ever taken a time-saving shower together in real life? I think the answer is to be late to class. No class is important enough to have a potentially scarring shower experience with your roommate.

—N, 28 (M)

THE SUPERYACHT

IN NEW ZEALAND, where I'm from, it's common to travel overseas after you've finished university. Most people don't have much professional experience yet, so they spend time working as a nanny or traveling. Working on a superyacht is also very popular, because it's tax-free money, and absolutely everything is paid for—from moisturizer and shampoo in the cupboard to every meal. Most boats have a cook just for the crew.

I traveled around Europe after I graduated, and got an apartment with a friend in the south of France. My friend got her boat job first, and it took me a few more weeks to get my job. I had absolutely no experience and completely made up my CV—I said I'd worked on a fishing yacht—because everyone else faked their résumés too.

I'd heard all these wonderful stories of people working on billionaires' boats, where they worked on the owner's third boat—one that was never used—so they got paid tons for not much work. I also had friends who worked on boats for several seasons, and they spent summers in the Mediterranean and winters in the Caribbean. Charter boats are the ideal, because if someone is renting a boat for a quarter of a million dollars, you assume they're going to tip incredibly well. You can work really hard for a week and get tipped tens of thousands of dollars. But boat owners don't tip. You have to take a leap of faith and hope you get a good boat.

The boat I worked on was owned by a wealthy man who worked in telecommunications, and it had thirteen crew members and could accommodate twelve guests. The cabins were all tiny double rooms with bunk beds. There was a cabin that fit three girls, but because the head stewardess hated me, she put me in a tiny room with a deckhand in his late thirties, instead of in the room with two other girls my age.

I couldn't tell my family about the situation until after I got off the boat—they would have been horrified that I was living with a guy in such close quarters when there was a spare bed elsewhere. The two of us had different shifts. I worked during the day and slept at night, and he was sometimes on watch at night and asleep during the day. There were a few times when I came into the room and his laptop was on, and it was obvious he was watching porn. Thankfully, he never masturbated while I was there, at least that I know of. It wasn't that he was gross, but he did make me uncomfortable—you don't get much privacy on a boat.

I got along well with the rest of the crew, which included a couple from New Zealand. No one hooked up on our boat—the men were older and the girls weren't interested. But on other boats, everyone has sex with everyone else. You earn so much money that you can afford to party and drink Moët. There's lots of cocaine on the fun boats.

My job was in the laundry room. In the five weeks I was on the boat, I only saw a guest once, and that was because he wandered into the kitchen by accident. Most of the time, I was below deck doing laundry, which included doing disgusting things like scrubbing the underwear of the Russian prostitute the owner had brought on board as his guest.

When the guests weren't on board and I was allowed above

deck, we cleaned the entire boat. Everyone had a tricked-out cleaning kit, with toothbrushes for scrubbing hard-to-get places and Q-tips to clean light fixtures. I picked up a lot of good tricks—if you put vinegar and water in a spray bottle, it's a great cleaning agent.

The boat itself traveled from Cannes to St. Tropez, and then to Portofino. Three days before we got to Venice, the head stewardess told me that my trial period was coming to an end and they couldn't hire me permanently. I was sick of it by then anyway, so I got off in Venice and happily moved to London. No matter how much money I make, I'll never own a boat. It's so expensive—even if you never take it anywhere, you still have to pay for the crew and maintenance. I haven't lived on a boat again since then or even been on a cruise.

—L, 28 (F)

THE RUSSIAN MISSIONARY

I GREW UP IN SALT LAKE CITY and was raised by a Catholic father and a nonpracticing Mormon mother. My parents have always been incredibly supportive of letting my brother and me decide what religion we wanted to follow on our own. After studying many different religions, I decided at sixteen that Mormonism is what I relate to the most. I became Mormon then, and it's been a huge part of my life ever since. In college, it was interesting to go from a place where everybody knows and understands what Mormonism is to a place where people asked, "Are you in a cult?" or "How many wives does your dad have?" It was a fun opportunity to talk to people about what being Mormon is actually like, instead of what most people think it's like.

After I graduated, I realized that there are very few truly liberal Mormons in the world. I thought it was worthwhile for people to meet more Mormons like me, as opposed to ones who have never left Salt Lake City, so I signed up to serve a mission. Young Mormons serve missions all over the world—you don't get to choose where you go, and it's always a bit of a gamble. You could go to Mozambique or Tulsa, Oklahoma. The one place I did not want to go was Russia, because I learned Russian in college and had lived there before. I remember praying, "God, I'll go wherever you want me to go, but if it's got to be Russia, then please not Moscow." It's a huge city, and it's dirty and loud, and people are mean—if you think New Yorkers are bad, Muscovites can be worse. And lo and behold, I was sent to Moscow.

Because I spoke the language, I didn't have to spend three months in the missionary training center learning how to teach in a new language. But in the eighteen months I served, each of my seven companions—the people with whom you live and work with for six weeks at a time—were native Russians, and only my last companion spoke English. I spent just under a year in Moscow, eight months in a city northeast of it called Yaroslavl, and a brief time in Kazakhstan. When you spend twenty-four hours a day seven days a week within sight and sound of a person you didn't choose to live with, you get all kinds of great stories.

Even before I met Sister Volkov, I had heard rumors about her. She had a reputation for being unmanageable and kind of bizarre. She was a stunning girl, but was very self-aware of her beauty. She had a pouch with twenty-seven different tubes of mascara in it, and she applied two coats of each every day. It took her three hours to get ready every morning, which meant she didn't always follow the Mormon handbook. The handbook, or the white bible, essentially tells you how to live your life. There's no argument as to what is right and what is wrong as a missionary, because part of the purpose is to learn obedience. According to the handbook, you have to be awake at six thirty, and pray and exercise for thirty minutes with your companion, and then come back, get dressed, have breakfast, and be ready to go for the day by eight. Sister Volkov took two or three hours every morning. She had really long hair, and in the twelve weeks we lived together, I only saw her wash her hair once. Every single morning was like prom—she went through tons of Aquanet a week creating these elaborate hairdos, and it was easier if her hair wasn't slick from showering.

Sister Volkov acted as if everyone loved her, which might

have been delusional. We started working together, and what her previous companion and the mission president neglected to tell me was that she had a horrible seizure disorder, which didn't manifest in a normal way. She didn't have seizures where she fell over and shook. Instead, she froze up—you could see her joints stiffen up—and it was totally terrifying. The first time it happened, we were on the subway and she stood completely still, and I thought she was going to fall over. She also didn't take her medication, because she didn't like the way she felt on it, so she was having more seizures where she was essentially blacking out and wouldn't remember what she was doing for the hour or so before her seizure.

As a teacher, she was great—she was good at improvisation, and so was I, so the two of us could essentially plan entire lessons in our heads. We worked really well together when it came to teaching. She also had a lot of poise and composure and was an amazing storyteller—she could transfix you with any story, including Mormon urban legends. People either loved her or hated her. The good thing about having two missionaries is that even if you hate one of them, you can still connect with the other person teaching you. A lot of people loved Sister Volkov, because she was incredibly dynamic and they never saw her awful side. When we were on trains, she was a total gross-Russian-guy magnet—she was everything a Russian guy wanted—and invariably found a group of guys playing cards and asked to play with them. She always cheated, which was funny.

In a good companionship, both people should always know what's going on. But Sister Volkov hid our cell phone from me—we only had one per companionship. She often disappeared into the bathroom with it and called people, and I was pretty sure she was calling home, which you're not supposed to do. One day, she told me she had a strong feeling she had to go to an area that wasn't technically in our mission boundaries. One of the things we value as Mormons is guidance by the spirit, and she forced me to go along with her. When we arrived, we turned a corner, and her father was standing there with things for her—it was obviously preplanned, and they clearly wanted to go to lunch together but didn't want me there. It was those types of things that bothered me—it wasn't what being a missionary was about. I didn't like her because she was so manipulative, which is the exact opposite of what you want when you're trying to communicate the most important thing in your life to others.

Thankfully, I saw other missionaries enough that I could bitch about Sister Volkov when I wanted to, especially because she didn't speak English. Many of the Russian missionaries did, so the Americans often got around that by speaking Pig Latin. I've learned that I can live through anything for six weeks, so the whole time, I kept thinking, *If I can get through six weeks, I'll be fine and will get transferred somewhere else*. When our six weeks were over, I thought I'd never see her again.

A few months later, I got a phone call from my mission president—this was incredibly rare, because usually we all had to go to a central building in Moscow where they announced transfers in a ceremonious way. I'd only spoken to my mission president a few times, and he called me and said he was going to tell me my next two transfers. "In February, you're going to Kazakhstan," he said. Kazakhstan is the holy grail for missionaries in my area. Everyone wanted to go because it is so nice there, and it's much easier to be a missionary in a place where people invite you in for dinner and offer to feed you. "But before that," the mission president said, "I'm sending you back to Yaroslavl to serve with Sister Volkov again." This was the period during Thanksgiving and Christmas, and Russians don't typically celebrate Christmas. It was freezing cold and as awful as I had envisioned. That winter was one of the coldest winters on record—it was negative three degrees Celsius almost every single day, and we were out on the streets walking around and talking to people the whole time. Meanwhile, I had decided that I wasn't going to talk to Sister Volkov.

The apartment we shared in Yaroslavl had two bedrooms. The handbook guidelines state that companions have to sleep in the same room, but not the same bed. All Russian furniture is convertible, so it looks like sitting room furniture during the day and someone can sleep on it at night. There was an Ikea bed in the room and a chair that folded up into a bed, and that's what I slept on for several months. We had a tiny kitchen and a bathroom. One of the few exceptions to the rule of being within sight and sound of each other at all times is when you're in the bathroom, which was often a refuge for missionaries. If you wanted to be alone, you locked yourself in the bathroom.

On the night before Christmas Eve, we were rushing home because the next day we were getting on a train to meet all the missionaries in Moscow to celebrate together. We were already super late because Sister Volkov had been dillydallying. We passed by a grocery store, and she said she wanted to go in. I asked her if she was hungry, but she simply said, "No, there's something I need to do." Even though we were already late and had to be up at four thirty in the morning, she insisted on making a stop. I told her I'd stand in the front and wait for her for five minutes. Since you're never supposed to leave your companion, this was something we often did as leverage—we forced the other to be disobedient if they wanted to do something that wasn't allowed.

Sister Volkov disappeared into the grocery store and came back with an armful of tacky Christmas tree ornaments and plastic snowflakes. I thought she had bought tacky gifts for the other sister missionaries, which was very Russian of her—Russians love tacky gifts. But we got back to our apartment, and she pulled out one of her four epic suitcases that weighed over a hundred pounds each, because Sister Volkov was a total shopaholic. She disappeared into another room and by then, it was getting late—we were supposed to be in bed by ten, but it was past midnight. And any time I couldn't see Sister Volkov, I would get nervous that she was having a seizure or that she'd fallen and hurt herself. Forty-five minutes later, she busted through the door with all the poise and grace of a 1930s dramatic actress, did a little turn, and said, "How do you like my holiday look?" She had taken the tacky ornaments and sewn them in the shape of a sash onto a summery sundress. She was always obsessed with her looks and wore ostentatious clothing in general, like a giant fur hat, which wasn't protocol for missionaries. We were there to be humble and work with people who are insanely poor, and we weren't supposed to wear anything over-the-top. She liked to dress up because she wanted others to tell her how great she looked. With the Christmas-ornament sundress, all I could think to say was, "Don't you think you'll be cold in that?" If I had thought about it more, I would have told her she looked incredible, so she would have worn it and it would have been hilarious. But I was mortified, because she was someone I was responsible for.

For some reason, my comment appealed to her—if I had told her she couldn't wear it or that she looked great, she would have worn it. So she went through her suitcases to find other things she could wear to the Christmas Eve party, which was a bunch of missionaries in a room eating food that someone else had cooked for them with meat and vegetables in it. Those were two things we never bought in Russia—I lived almost entirely on buckwheat groat and crappy bread while I was there. I used to dream of salads, and whenever I left the country to renew my visa, I came back with cans of chickpeas. It was pretty pathetic.

Sister Volkov was atrocious to me over the course of the holidays, and later that week, after we'd gone eight days without speaking to each other, we were coming back from a baptism—a rare occasion for us. Missionaries who live in Brazil will probably baptize somewhere from one hundred to two hundred people they teach over the course of their mission, but in Russia, you're lucky if one person gets baptized. We were walking back very late, and it was dark outside—there are not a lot of lights on the street in Yaroslavl. All of a sudden, I could tell that she was going to have a seizure—she was walking more slowly for no reason, and Sister Volkov is a woman who walks with a lot of purpose. The only time she slowed down was if she was looking at a weird trinket that somebody was selling on the side of the road. I turned around and I could see she was about to fall over. I ran over, put my arms around her, and held onto her in the dark and freezing cold. The only thing I could think to do was to say her first name—which we never used—over and over. I don't even think she knew what my first name was. I kept holding her and saying, "Antonia, it's okay. It's okay." This was a person who I had so much hatred for, but standing there and knowing the only thing I could do for her was to hold on to her was so personal and intimate. It was such a revealing moment for me, and I was overcome with a strong feeling of love for a person who made my life hellish for twelve weeks. I could tell when the seizure was over because her joints softened and her muscles relaxed. She woke up, stood up on her own, and in a classic Sister Volkov way, looked at me and said, "Why are you stopping? We're late." It was a quick jolt back to reality.

After my mission ended, I stayed in touch with all my companions except Sister Volkov. We talked almost every week, and most have come to visit me. Then in 2010, the Mormon church opened a temple in Kiev, Ukraine, which was a big deal because there are churches everywhere, but only 140 temples in the world, and before that, Mormons from Russia and Ukraine had to go to Korea or Finland to go to a temple. I traveled to Kiev for the dedication, and it was incredibly exciting. I saw all these people I had taught, and in the distance, I saw Sister Volkov. She'd gotten married, and I looked at her and smiled and said hello, although I didn't stop and talk to her because she was distracted by someone else.

Later, a friend who had served in my mission came up to me and said, "Did you see that Sister Volkov is here?" "Yes," I said, "I waved and said hi." He had been chatting with Sister Volkov, and when he asked if she'd seen me yet, she'd said, "Who is that? Is she American?" And my friend was flabbergasted—he didn't want to say, "Yes, you served twelve weeks with her." It was almost funny—she's the one person from our mission who I can never forget, and I don't even exist in her mind anymore.

—E, 29 (F)

RECENT GRADS

THE FOUR-MONTH HANGOVER

AFTER COLLEGE GRADUATION, my best friend from high school and I decided to move in together in New York. We knew it would be cheaper if we found a three-bedroom, so Dave suggested we bring along his college friend Jimmy. I'd met Jimmy at parties over the last few years, and I always thought he was a fun guy. Everything was fine for about six weeks, and then Jimmy started to become very withdrawn and paranoid and solemn.

We had a great first-floor apartment with a backyard and a nice big living area. Jimmy's bedroom was the one that faced the backyard. He would get upset if people were smoking out there or making noise after ten P.M. And he tied this all to his ongoing health problems. He's a good-looking guy but very frail. Apparently, he was a football player in high school, but developed a muscular dystrophy disease, which left him weak. He claimed to have incredibly fragile health, and that any cigarette smoke coming in through the window would send him into a death spiral. He was very, very dramatic about it and spent most of his time in his bedroom. The only time I ever saw him was when he was on a cocaine binge—which probably contributed to his bad health.

It was a hot summer, and his window had flat bars on it so he couldn't put an air conditioner in the window. He bought a ridiculous stand-up air conditioner that didn't work at all, was sweating all the time and miserable from the heat, and got sicker and angrier. It got to the point where he started to look like a vicious vampire or alien—whenever he emerged from the bedroom, he'd slink around the corner and hug the wall, trying not to make eye contact when he went to the bathroom and back. It became increasingly terrifying, and you could never tell if he was home or asleep, because the door was always shut. We never knew how to behave in our own space. Whether we could relax or not depended on if he was there.

One day he came home and called an apartment meeting, and told Dave and me that he'd been getting tests done to figure out why he was feeling so bad. The doctor had told him that he had some sort of extremely rare degenerative muscle disease—and that he'd be dead within the year. Needless to say, we were shocked and said we'd do anything we could to help out. He told us he was still going for more tests, and he started making pot brownies all the time, because marijuana was the one thing that made him feel better. And when he made the brownies, he baked like he was mad at the stove. He was a terrible baker who angrily stirred saucepans full of butter and never cleaned it up afterward. It was like he was disgusted by the whole operation but was doing it anyway because he'd convinced himself it was for its medical properties. Meanwhile, he was still doing a lot of coke. He told us that it was important for him to get sleep, and that the heat was debilitating for him. His main symptom was that he couldn't move for hours on end, because he was so afflicted by lethargy that he could barely get out of bed unless he was stoned or on cocaine.

Jimmy kept getting worse and worse, and we had no idea what was going on. We were absolutely terrified and trying to be nice to him, but Dave and I were privately asking ourselves,

Why aren't his parents coming out here and taking him home? If he was dying, shouldn't he be with his parents instead of living in New York? He'd gotten a job but quit because he was so tired all the time, so he was spending his parents' money lying around in bed getting stoned—which actually is not different from many others who have recently graduated from college and are living in New York.

But he stuck around, and finally he told us, good news—he wasn't dying. He just had a horrible crippling muscular disease that meant he would never feel good again. But after the whole "I'm dying" thing, we were like, that's great! We were still trying to be supportive and offered to pick up his medication for him. I've known several people who are sick, like teenagers with severe arthritis who are in pain all the time but are still the sunniest, friendliest people in the world. I've never met anyone who was crueler or nastier than Jimmy. The worse he felt, the meaner he was. He had a passive-aggressive way of leaving a voice mail yelling at us about something we'd done wrong—such as grinding coffee in the morning and waking him up—but only after we were out of the house and on the subway. For a while, these angry voice mails were the only way he communicated.

He also screamed at my then girlfriend, now wife, because she once finished his orange juice. He made a huge deal about how difficult it was for him to get out of bed, and that buying the orange juice took all of the energy he had for the day. He absolutely hated our girlfriends.

The worst part was Dave and Jimmy actually lived together in college. I found out afterward that they'd lived in a big group for several years, six or seven guys in a suite, so they didn't notice each other's weirdness as much. But before the three of us moved in together, every one of Dave's friends had told him not to move in with Jimmy because he was crazy.

I finally went out of town for a week, and was so relieved to be away from Jimmy. My younger brother was coming to stay with us for five days after I went out of town, and to put it nicely, my brother is not a sensitive guy. He's hilarious and a lot of fun, but can be incredibly rude.

Without asking anyone, my brother decided to have a party at our apartment and invite his college friends via Facebook. It was pretty inconsiderate, so this was actually a reasonable thing for Jimmy to be mad about. He called me while I was on vacation, and you know that feeling where you're fighting with someone, and you see their name come up on your phone, and your stomach immediately contracts? I felt this way about Jimmy all the time. He called and ranted about my brother, and I said I'd solve the problem, that the party wouldn't happen at our house, but he kept sending me angry texts all weekend.

I came back from my vacation, and Jimmy was already pissed off that my brother was there. In addition to being insensitive, my brother is also a terrible houseguest. He wasn't bathing a lot, and left his stuff everywhere. Dave and I had spent a summer dancing around Jimmy, trying to be sweet and nonconfrontational. But my brother was loud, smelly, and messy, and gave Jimmy a lot of shit. He knew the whole backstory of Jimmy being sick, but didn't care at all. Jimmy sent me another one of those angry voice mails, with a long litany of complaints, ranging from the reasonable (your brother left his crap everywhere) to slightly paranoid (he was so smelly that he stunk up the sofa, so I had to pay to dry clean it). He said the smell was making him physically sick, and he did what he often did and stayed in a hotel for two days without telling us. Once he came back, he told us that he couldn't handle it anymore and was moving home. I'd never been happier that my brother was an asshole.

Dave and I were ecstatic. We knew what date he was moving out, and so we purposefully tried to avoid being there while his parents were there. But I ended up in the house as his family was coming in, and when I said hi to his mom to be friendly, she gave me this horrible look, as if I were a war criminal who had tortured her baby.

We later found out that Jimmy was never sick—he never had anything physically wrong with him and it was completely psychosomatic. He was essentially hungover for about four months, but told us he was dying! Dave and I both had nightmares about him for months afterward, where we dreamed he'd come back to the apartment and we offended him somehow, and he was creeping up on us like a vampire. It was like a bad breakup, except I never liked him.

After Jimmy moved out, we had a "house-falling" party. That was my idea, because it had been a Cold War for those four months and felt like the Berlin Wall had come down. We stayed in the apartment, and another good friend of ours from high school moved into that room. The thing is, he became depressed too—maybe the room itself was cursed.

—W, 26 (M)

THE PERSISTENT PESTS

WHEN I FIRST MOVED to Philadelphia for a job, I lived in an apartment with three others. The lease was up that summer, and two of them, who were dating, decided it was time to find their own spot, as did the third roommate, who had been there for three years and was ready to leave. I wanted to keep the place, because it was nice, huge, in a good area, and priced way cheaper than anything else. I looked at other apartments as alternatives, but they were about three hundred dollars more a month—it would have been an expensive move.

All of a sudden, I had to find three normal strangers to live with (and fast, because if I didn't have roommates locked down, my landlord was going to start showing the place, and I knew it'd go quickly). Luckily, my sister goes to school in Philadelphia, and she had a friend who was looking for a place with two others. They came and saw the place, liked it, and said they wanted to move in. Given the alternative—recruiting three non–serial killers off the Internet in a couple days—I said it was fine.

At the beginning of September, all three of them moved in and were living in the apartment part-time. My sister's friend Jill was doing a clinical rotation in Delaware and wasn't around much. The two others, Tasha and Dana, worked part-time at home and were looking for full-time work in the city. They went home for weekends because they worked there, and then came back during the week for a couple of days. Because they were only at the apartment part-time, they didn't sign the lease on time. The three girls paid the first month's rent, but were late on the security deposit and last month's rent.

The first thing that happened after they moved in was that we started noticing fleas, which may have been left over from a previous roommate's cat. I had little bite marks on my arms, and the fleas were hard to get rid of. We had an exterminator come in and bomb the place, but the fleas didn't all die immediately. There were some leftover ones hopping around for a couple days after the exterminator came.

I did some research on what fleas and bedbugs look like to figure out which they were—I did not want them to be bedbugs. The flea infestation had finally died down when, all of a sudden, one Monday night, I saw what I identified as a bedbug on my wall. I had been telling my friends, "Thank god these were fleas and not bedbugs." One of the Web sites even said, count your lucky stars if you have fleas and not bedbugs because they're a lot easier to get rid of. As soon as we got rid of the fleas, I saw a bedbug.

I went upstairs that night and slept on the couch. The next morning, I called the same exterminator and he said, "Yeah, you've got them." He had all these guidelines on what we had to do to get rid of them, and I was totally demoralized. We'd just had one bug issue and now we had another that was infinitely worse. None of my roommates were there at the time, on Tuesday morning, but I texted them to say, "So you know, we have bedbugs, the exterminator came, and he'll be coming back later this week. Let me know what day would be best next week because we can't be in the apartment when they're treating it."

Tasha texted me back immediately and said something like,

"Take my name off the lease, I'm moving out." I called her back and said, "That's not how it works. If you want to move out, that's fine, but you need to find someone to replace you and take over your portion of the lease—you can't break a twelve-month lease three weeks in."

Two minutes later, she texted again: "I'm moving out, and my dad's getting a lawyer." I didn't know her very well at this point, and I didn't know if this was a temper tantrum that would boil over. I was too busy dealing with getting our apartment ready for the exterminator. There are all these things you have to do, including taking every picture off the wall, throwing out box springs, removing mattresses from frames, washing every piece of clothing in hot water, and dousing all suitcases in Lysol. And every single thing had to go in a trash bag—there were bags all over the apartment with all my stuff. I was starting the process in my room downstairs, and suddenly I heard movement upstairs, though I was the only person at home. Tasha had barged into the apartment with her parents—they'd essentially left home as soon as she'd sent me that text—and started moving her stuff out.

The first thing I said to her parents was, "Are you sure you want to move this stuff out now? We're getting treated for bedbugs on Friday, and you could be taking the bedbugs home with you." I even suggested that if Tasha wanted to move out, she could leave her things here, get them exterminated, and then take them. I figured that was a rational thing to say. But that opened the floodgates for her parents to start screaming at me and blaming me for everything from fleas to bedbugs to the apartment's general state of cleanliness.

Meanwhile, I wasn't even the landlord—I was a tenant, like their daughter, and dealing with the problem too. It was bad enough I had bedbugs to deal with, but now I also had these crazy angry parents yelling at me. They went as far as to accuse me of knowing about the bedbugs beforehand, and only revealing them the day after their daughter had signed the lease—as if it was a choice of mine to lie in a pool of blood-sucking insects for any longer than necessary. That's what really blew me away.

Her dad kept screaming at me and saying, "If we have to see you again, we'll see you in court." I don't know what they would have sued me for, but he said the bedbugs were cause for termination of the lease. And then he followed up with, "But it doesn't matter because she's not on the lease." Which was not true, since she'd signed it the day before. I finally got tired of the yelling and went back downstairs, and when they left, her dad took the lease with them—probably to destroy it so there was no proof his daughter's name was ever on it.

During that week, I was the only person in the apartment getting it ready for the bedbug treatments. One of the things you have to do is buy a mattress encaser, and I offered to purchase them for Jill and Dana if they paid me back. Dana, who had previously hinted that she wanted to buy a new mattress, wouldn't give me a straight answer. I wanted to call her and say, "Listen, I know it's annoying that you have to make one multiple-choice decision here, but I've taken two days off of work to get ready for the exterminator." Eventually she told me to throw her mattress away. She didn't have many clothes or other stuff, but I also had to empty all the drawers and bookcases because the bugs can get into wooden drawers. There wasn't much in the other rooms, but Dana did have a bong, which I didn't want the exterminator seeing. I finally found a shoebox to put it in, but that was the extent of what I had to do to get her room ready—throw her mattress away and hide her bong.

Dana and Tasha were very close, so I figured that after the whole Tasha blowup Dana was probably out too. I talked to Jill that night, and she said she would stay. She too had called her dad to ask what to do, and he said, "Well, you get rid of the bedbugs and pay the next month's rent." It reassured my faith in humanity a bit that there was a parent out there who knew what a contract was.

The next day, Dana texted me to say she was also moving out. She and her mom arrived Monday to pack up, and it wasn't quite the tornado that the first incident was. Her mom said there was a big upholstered chair in the room they didn't want to take, and asked if I'd take care of it. I basically said, "No, if you want to take it out to the Dumpster or the curb, go ahead." I went out for a jog, and when I got back, they were standing by the car looking like they were done. I wished them good luck, and said, "Did you take care of the chair?" And they hadn't. First they said they didn't have room for it, to which I replied, "That's not my issue, you're moving out and it's your responsibility to take your stuff with you." Then she said it might have bedbugs on it. "Yes, so does everything else in your car," I said. Finally she turned to her daughter, said, "Let's go," and got in the car and drove away.

After the two of them left, I put the apartment on Craigslist to find new roommates. Someone moved in less than a week later. I told him we'd recently been exterminated for bedbugs, because he deserved to know. The biggest endorsement of the apartment's buglessness was that I was still living there. My exterminator told me everyone in Philadelphia knows someone who's had bedbugs—it's one of the most bedbug-infested cities in the country. But no one talks about it.

While the ordeal was happening, I alternated between sleeping on the couch and staying with a girl I'd just started seeing. I had debated whether to tell her about the fleas, and then a week later, had to tell her about the bedbugs. We'd only been on a few dates at that point, but I had to swear I wasn't sprouting bugs out of my armpits. She very graciously put me up for a few nights that first week. And on top of that, there was insane drama at work—my boss was fired. I kept waiting for a cameraman to pop his head up somewhere and tell me I was on some type of reality show.

—C, 27 (M)

THE ROOMMATES WITH BENEFITS

AFTER THREE MONTHS of subletting an apartment in Austin, I started looking on Craigslist for a place to rent. I'd seen a couple of places I didn't love when I met Diane, a twenty-eight-year-old who owned a house. The day I went to visit, Jake, who had already been living in the house for about a year, was there too, and the three of us got along pretty well. It was a three-bedroom ranch house with a pool in the backyard and was in a nice neighborhood—or so I thought at the time.

My room was empty because the girl who had lived there had moved to Europe. I thought it was a good sign that the last tenant hadn't left because she was sick of the roommates. Since my sublet was ending, I moved in within the week. At the time, I was working as a nanny and had weird hours. Jake was an ex-marine taking classes and Diane was a quiet girl with a nine-to-five job, so our schedules were all different. We saw one another at night sometimes, but once in a while days went by without us seeing each other. There was never any fighting over the bathroom, and we were social—Jake and I hung out by the pool and the three of us had dinner together if we were all home at the same time.

One day, at eight in the morning, I woke up to the sound of glass breaking. I thought one of my housemates had dropped a glass until I heard stumbling around. I didn't think either of them would be drunkenly breaking glasses on the floor in the morning and I sensed something wasn't right, so I went to investigate.

As soon as I walked out of my room, I saw a guy standing there covered in blood. He'd used his forearm to break the window above our kitchen sink and had probably hoisted himself up through it using our patio furniture. Since this was a ranch house, there was only one floor. The intruder was a total crackhead, and as I was screaming at him and chasing him out of the house, he grabbed my DVD player and cable box and walked out. I think he was planning to take more, but I scared him away. I don't know if he was armed—he never showed me a weapon. It sounds braver than it was, but I was the only one home.

I called 911 and told them my house had been broken into. "I can see the guy walking down the street with my DVD player in one arm and cable box in the other," I said. The dispatcher asked if anyone else was in the house and told me to wait outside in my front yard. I was standing there waiting when the dispatcher said, "Ma'am, do you mind if we apprehend him first? We see him down the block from you."

After they caught him, the cops came back to my house and were talking to me when Jake rode up on his bicycle. Something was clearly wrong, because there were six cop cars outside, a CSI team fingerprinting everything in the house, and blood everywhere in the kitchen. I was telling Jake about the break-in and how the police were bringing our things back when the cops asked us if we had any weapons in the house. "Kitchen knives?" I replied. And Jake casually said, "Yes, I have six guns in the house, do you want to see my permit?" I had no idea there were guns in the house. The cops turned to him and said, "I wish you had been home so you could have shot this guy." I couldn't believe I was living in this crazy state. Diane was still at work, so

Jake and I cleaned up the fingerprint powder and blood, which took forever.

The next weekend, Jake took me to the range to teach me how to shoot. He told me I needed to learn how to shoot a couple of his guns. As an ex-marine he knew how to handle guns well, and also collected them for fun. He hadn't been trying to hide the guns; it was something that never came up in everyday conversation. We spent the day at the range, and after that, started hanging out more and more, and eventually started hooking up.

Our relationship was always very casual, and Diane either never knew or never acknowledged it. At night, I went into his room, or he came into mine, to see if the other was up for hanging out. The other person could always say, "not tonight," and it was fine. We essentially became roommates with benefits and hooked up for eight months. We didn't hang out much outside of the house, but he did meet my parents when they came to visit once—as a roommate, not a boyfriend. We went to the movies occasionally if neither of us were doing anything. We both knew we had a good thing going and didn't want to mess it up with a big discussion about our feelings.

We were hooking up exclusively until I started dating another guy, and then we ended things amicably. We both moved out eventually—Jake went to hike the Appalachian Trail, and I left for law school. As for the intruder, he's serving ten years in prison—after all, it was Texas and he was on private property. He apparently had a long record. Every time he wasn't in jail, he was breaking into someone else's house.

—E, 27 (F)

THE PSEUDO-FRAT

I STARTED DATING COLIN in London when we were both studying abroad. After we finished our senior years at our respective colleges, I made plans to move to New York, where he was. We never discussed moving in together, but he was the only person I knew there. He told me not to sign a lease, and that we should live together for a couple of months and see where we were. I had a few friends who I knew were moving to New York later, so I figured I could move in with them at some point.

When I first moved into his apartment, there were five guys living there. Three of us shared a bedroom with bunk beds. My boyfriend and I slept on the top bunk, and a friend of his slept on the bottom. My dresses and shirts were all stored in the kitchen cabinets. I was barely at the apartment, but when I was there, I needed quick access to my clothes. Getting ready quickly for my fashion magazine job and my nighttime bar job was practically impossible. I was always running around the city like a chicken with its head cut off, with no idea where I was, but still trying to look cute and impressive and stylish for my internship. It was a nightmare to try and get readjusted to my new life and come home to five screaming boys playing Battlestar Galactica or blowing up zombies over and over again. And because the boys were moving out of the apartment at the end of the summer, they trashed it.

When the lease ended, Colin and I decided to move in together. It was out of necessity, convenience, and a desire to play house. It felt romantic but was ultimately ill-fated. We found an apartment that was so close to the old one that we walked our things over—the mattress was wheeled a few blocks down on a skateboard. We were living in Alphabet City, in a one-bedroom apartment with a balcony in a freshly redone building. We each paid $1,500 a month, and I was an intern with a part-time bar job. I was really frustrated that his parents helped him out and he didn't have to support himself financially, and that put a wedge between us. We also got a cat, which was a horrible idea—she hated both of us.

We were in the apartment for nine months when I started feeling really smothered and going a little crazy. I had been working at a full-time job for two months and was finally starting to feel like I was getting a grip on the city. I had my own friends from work, and thought I finally had a life separate from Colin and his friends. I started looking for my own apartment, and thought maybe I'd move out but we'd stay together. One Friday at work, we were chatting online, casually talking about how much distance there was between us. "Maybe we should break up," I said, because I was resentful and mad. And in a weird twist of fate, he said, "Yeah, you're totally right." I backpedaled immediately, said I was sorry and didn't mean it, but he knew I'd been hinting at it for a while. He didn't come home all weekend, and I didn't call him—it didn't feel real to me. I thought we were playing break up, the way we were playing house when we lived together. But when I saw him again, he told me he was staying in the apartment and I should move out. The next day, he got on a plane home to California, where he stayed for a month until after I was gone.

Since Colin was away, I hunted for a new apartment and moved out on my own. My cousin and his best friend had recently graduated—they were two straight musical theater majors—and were moving to New York. And again, out of convenience, but also the need to be around someone supportive, I agreed to move in with them. We found a three-bedroom apartment in Brooklyn, and I spent the whole summer there by myself before they moved in. I got to do whatever I wanted, including walking around naked. It was bliss.

Then the two of them moved in and since I was living with two men, it felt like I was back where I started. They didn't just watch TV—they sang the commercials. They thought it was hilarious to sing sad songs from *Les Misérables* while they cut onions. Hailing a cab meant repurposing songs from *Cat on a Hot Tin Roof*, and Sunday mornings were spent washing dishes to Mandy Patinkin singing "Finishing the Hat" from *Sunday in the Park with George*. I had no peace at all. It wasn't as bad as five different guys, but it was like I was living in a musical. They also had video game parties all night and bizarre bongs everywhere. My cousin and I grew up together and are very close, but when we were living together, we weren't as close because he was always in the middle. I felt like I'd outgrown living with boys—I was living in a frat house when I wanted to be building a life of my own. Some people say men are easy to live with—they're not emotional, they won't borrow your clothes, they don't turn things into drawn-out emotional arguments. But that wasn't the case at all. They were so emotional and passive-aggressive that I didn't know how to deal with them.

Two years later, they've moved out, and two girls have taken over. We've turned it into a lovely lady palace, where everyone is grown-up and independent. We have separate lives, and it's not that we don't like one another, we're just never around at the same time. I'm hoping this is the happy end of my roommate story.

—G, 27 (F)

THE PASSIVE-AGGRESSIVE PIG

I FOUND A ROOMMATE ON KIJIJI, the Canadian version of Craigslist, for the extra den that my roommate Tara and I wanted to rent out. Our new roommate, Kate, seemed totally nice during the interview—she was a year older than us and worked in advertising. We specifically didn't want to rent to students, and since she had a good job, she seemed legit.

We had never rented anything out before, and most of the problems that occurred were because we didn't have proper documentation. Our rent was due on the first, but Kate never paid us on the day of. We should have asked her for postdated checks, but we always had to remind her, and she always said, okay, remind me tomorrow. With cable bills, she rounded down because it was never an even number. Forty-four dollars became forty dollars, which is not a big deal, but between cable, utilities, and rent, it added up. Every time, Kate said, "I'll get you later, I don't have any change right now." And I never got that money back.

We soon found out that she was incredibly dirty—there's a difference between messy and dirty, and she was dirty. There were black fingerprints on her white door. Tara and Kate shared a bathroom, and Tara is a total clean freak. Any time anyone comes over and uses the bathroom, she'll Lysol the entire toilet afterward. On the subway, Tara never holds the handrails. She was wearing a dress once and sat down, and her butt accidentally touched the subway seat. She had a panic attack and actually sprayed Lysol on her butt afterward. So Tara and Kate were complete, complete opposites. But Tara got so fed up that she stopped cleaning. At some point, there was an entire carpet of hair in the bathroom. The kitchen was gross too—all the door handles were greasy, including the microwave and fridge. And throughout the year, Kate never took out the trash, except for once when her sister was there. I should've gotten a security deposit for her room, because we had to steam clean the carpet, which turned from white to black.

Our relationship got worse as we started to realize how incompatible we were. Kate stopped making any effort about six months in. We saw dirty underwear on the floor and dishes in the bed. The dishes piled up in her room—we often looked in the cabinet and realized there were no dishes left, because they were all in her room. Sometimes she put the dishes in the sink, but they were never clean. We washed most of her dishes—it always came down to whoever had the lower tolerance.

When she moved in, we were friendly. We always said, if you ever need milk, borrow it. Though she drank our juice and used our cooking supplies, we were never allowed to use anything of hers. She even told one of my friends she wasn't allowed to sit on the couch because it belonged to her.

A friend of mine stayed over once, and while we were at work, she decided to bake. She accidentally used Kate's butter—there wasn't a lot left and she finished it. I didn't have time to tell Kate that we'd used up her butter. But Kate dug through the trash and found the wrapper, and stuck it on the fridge door with a Post-it note that said, "This is my butter!!!" I still have a picture of it.

When her lease was up, she refused to move out at first,

probably because she was getting a great deal on rent. On her last day, she dragged it out as long as she could. She kept saying she had the right to stay until the last minute. At eleven thirty P.M., I blew up and started moving her stuff into the hallway. Kate and Tara were screaming at each other, because Kate still owed Tara money. I threw the last of her stuff out of the apartment and slammed the door in her face, and that's how we ended things. We later found out she'd moved downstairs to the fifth floor, because she'd made another friend in the building. Whenever we saw her afterward, we pretended we didn't know her.

—J, 27 (F)

THE TEENAGE PROTECTOR

I WAS TWENTY-FIVE and just starting my career when my aunt offered me an incredible living situation. She had found a two-story townhouse with three bedrooms, a washer-dryer, a living room, and a dining room. My eighteen-year-old cousin was heading to college in the same city and my aunt didn't want him to be alone and unsupervised, so she came up with the idea of pairing us up as roommates so that I would be somewhat of a big sister or guardian type. My cousin and I were close when we were young, but I hadn't spent much time with him in six years. I didn't know if I was supposed to be babysitting him or allowing him to have alcohol. I told him that if he was drinking, I didn't want to be anywhere near it—it was an awkward position to be in.

The house was set up so that my cousin and I both had rooms on the second floor, and we used the extra room as an office and gym. He was a sloth who slept all day, and ate nothing but crackers, Cheez Whiz, and maybe a little piece of salami. I was always trying to get him to eat some real food, but he was never interested in going out to dinner.

Our next-door neighbors were a married couple in their late twenties with two kids. One night a few months into living together, I came home and saw the husband hanging out with my cousin and his friends downstairs. I chatted with them briefly before heading upstairs to my room, and suddenly noticed the husband following me up the steps. We were at the top of the stairs when I told him he needed to leave. I saw his eyes darting around to the open door to my cousin's room, and he started trying to push me in. I was screaming and holding on to the doorframe for dear life, and eventually managed to push him backward with my butt. When he realized he wasn't going to be able to push me into the room, he went running down the stairs and out the door. I'm pretty sure he was on some kind of drugs at the time—afterward, he claimed he was drunk.

I had run into my room and locked my door when my cousin came knocking to ask if I was okay. I told him what had happened, and he followed the husband home and beat him up—he actually broke his hand on the guy's face. At the same time my cousin was beating this guy up, the wife came over to ask me what had happened. She was someone I was friendly with, so I told her what had happened, and she was completely incredulous.

I went to my boyfriend's place that night, and called the police the next day to file a report. I thought I would file a sexual assault report, but they told me I couldn't because I didn't actually have any wounds or bruises from the assault. I thought I might have some on my arms because he was trying to bear hug me as he was pushing me into the room, but it was nothing major. "I don't think you can file charges," the police said. "That guy's face is more evidence against your cousin. If you file charges, he might file against your cousin." The cops weren't very useful.

My cousin might have been young, but he was a good kid who stood up for me. We both knew the husband wouldn't bother us after that. When the landlord heard what had happened and saw the guy's face, she kicked both the neighbors and my cousin out of the building.

After all this, I wanted to hug my cousin. He felt like a brother to me, and I was horrified that he had broken his hand. Afterward, I always felt indebted to him. We don't live in the same place anymore—that little kid who never wanted to eat real food actually went to culinary school and became a sushi chef. The scars on his hand from beating the guy up are now nothing compared to the scars and burns he has from cooking. The funny thing is, my aunt thought I'd be the one to protect my cousin, but he's the one who came to my rescue that fateful night.

—K, 33 (F)

THE HEIST

MY BOYFRIEND CHRIS and I had been dating for about a year when we decided to move in together. At that point, I thought we were going to have a future with each other—he had even given me a promise ring. We found a two-level home, with two bedrooms and one and a half bathrooms. It was a nice space, just not in a very good neighborhood. When we moved in, I paid for all the furniture and appliances, because I made more money than he did.

Three or four months in, Chris broke up with me. I decided to move out, and he planned to move in with his best friend, Zach, but Zach took over my room in the apartment instead.

A month after I moved out, I got a phone call from Zach, who told me my ex had been cheating on me the entire time we were together. "He brought her over to my place all the time," he said. "All those times Chris said he was coming over to hang out with me and drink, he was actually hanging out with her." When Zach moved into the apartment, their rule was that this girl wouldn't hang out around the house, because Zach hated her. She was younger and just out of high school, and Chris had dated her briefly before the two of us got together. But Chris broke that rule immediately, and that girl became his new girlfriend. Zach and I hadn't been close at all—he called because he thought

Chris was being a douchebag. Plus, he wanted to get back at him for choosing the girl over their friendship.

When I moved out, I had left all the appliances I'd bought with him—the washer, the dryer, the fridge. Chris was supposed to pay me back over time, plus he owed me money on top of that: down payment on the car, his share of the rent and utility bills for multiple months, vacation expenses, the deposit for the apartment—it was a lot.

Zach and I hatched a plan: we were going to move all my appliances out while Chris wasn't home. We both knew Chris had no intention of paying me back any of the money he owed me. In order to protect myself from additional financial stress, I decided to take what I could and sell them to get some of my money back. When we got there, his new girlfriend was at the house. She called the cops on us, even though we had every right to be there. It was my property, and Zach had a key to the place. When the cops showed up, the girlfriend told them they were taking her stuff. "Actually," I said, "it's all mine." And the cops took my side. "All we can do is supervise while they move the stuff out," they said. I was able to get all my stuff back and move the appliances to my new place. I later went to Chris's workplace and took my car back too, while he was at work.

After I took the car, Chris came to my apartment because he wanted the things that were still in the car. He called the cops on me, so I had to empty the car of his things. He threatened to sue me to get the car back, but never did. I sold the washer and dryer on Craigslist. As for the fridge, I left it sitting in their backyard. When I went back to get it, Zach said someone had taken it away. Whether or not that's true, I have no idea. Chris has tried to contact me again since then, but I still won't speak to him.

—G, 29 (F)

THE MORMON HOUSEHOLD

LIKE MANY PEOPLE, I moved to New York for a job. But unlike most, I found my roommates through a friend, one I had met on the subway eight months prior when I was in New York for an internship. The two of us had kept in touch, and when I was moving back, she sent me an apartment listing from a listserv she was on. I didn't get a chance to see the place, but I trusted her judgment. I got in touch with a girl named Sarah, whose name was on the lease, who told me I'd be sharing a room with another girl. I lived at home during college, so I'd never shared a room, or even had a roommate, in my life. At twenty-eight, I wasn't sure if I could share a room with someone, but I knew I had to adapt in order to live in New York.

I arrived at the apartment late at night and met Sarah, who ran me through the apartment guidelines—don't leave food out, don't leave things in the common area, and so on—which I was perfectly fine with. Then she started talking about churches and wards, and I gave her a totally blank stare. I knew my friend was Mormon, and I knew the listserv was Mormon-based, but I had no idea that everyone who lived in the apartment was Mormon. And I don't think they were aware that I wasn't Mormon. Sarah was going on and on about which ward I should go to when I told her I wasn't Mormon. "Oh," she said with a bewildered look. "We won't worry about that right now."

I left my things out in the living room and went into my room, which had one lofted bed and a normal bed below it. They looked like bunk beds, but they were full-size. It was late and I was exhausted, so I went to bed, even though there were tons of things going through my head—what had I gotten myself into? I had seen photos of the place, but I didn't know the size of the room. The beds essentially took up the entire room and there wasn't much space to walk around. I had come from a two-story house in Texas where I had the entire upper floor to myself, because my brother was away at college, with an office, a bedroom, a media room, my own bathroom, and a walk-in closet.

My new roommate, Carrie, was a beautician ten years my junior—she's become a little sister to me. She had moved into the apartment a few weeks earlier. There are six of us total living in a four-bedroom apartment with three bathrooms, and I'm the only non-Mormon. The oldest roommate is forty-two and divorced—she had four children by the time she was twenty-four, because Mormons marry young and she had her kids back-to-back. There's also a thirty-three-year-old yoga teacher and a girl from Wisconsin who is an absolute sweetheart. She does more household work than anyone else and is very motherly. Most of them are converts—only one came from a big Mormon family.

Carrie has her quirks like everyone else. I know she can't do anything about the noise she makes when she tosses and turns in her sleep—that's part of sharing a room. When I want to go out, she offers to fix my hair or pick out a lipstick for me. Living with her is great, because I didn't grow up with a sister, and I became attached to her. I'm a photographer and I asked Carrie and her boyfriend to model for me so I could get some fresh work on my Web site. Little did I know, her boyfriend had decided to propose during the shoot, which was incredible. Carrie told me that the proposal was even more special because I was there. The age difference between us makes it hard, but it isn't anything I can't live with.

There are certain things I've had to get used to in a Mormon household—I've never been a big coffee drinker, but there's no Coke, coffee, or tea allowed in the house. And all my roommates have special garments they wear, similar to a slip with cap sleeves. The garments come in all types of materials and are sacred. They're worn underneath their clothes—even bras go over them. They go to church for three hours, and they don't shop on Sundays, so they buy everything they need on the other days. I've even started seeing similarities between Mormonism and my religion, Catholicism. At the end of the day, we're all still girls who experience the same things. We'll gossip when someone brings over a boy, even though we know they're not having sex because Mormons don't have sex until they get married. Learning all these things has been interesting. I've never seen the musical *The Book of Mormon*, which everyone says is awesome, but maybe if I had, I wouldn't have been so taken aback by all this when I first moved in.

The apartment works well because we all lead our own individual lives. Once in a while, we all sit down and eat together as a family on Sundays, which is great. I'm the first non-Mormon to live in the apartment, and once, Sarah said to me, "If you weren't so cool, I don't think you'd still be living here because you're not Mormon." The next day, one of my roommates said, "I can't believe those words came out of her mouth. Weren't you offended?" I didn't think much of it, because the things Sarah says don't affect me much. I signed a contract and pay rent, and nowhere in the contract did it say I had to be Mormon to live there. The more I get to know Sarah, the more I dislike her. She's not someone I want to be friends with—she's basically a landlady running a dorm of sorts. She makes so much money off of our rent that she's always traveling around the world. But the other girls are so easygoing and we all get along great. That's what makes living there bearable, since I know I'm overpaying.

For my next apartment, I'd love to have my own room. But if the rent was good and I really liked my roommate and found an awesome one-bedroom, I would be okay with sharing again. After all, I don't have anything to hide.

—J, 29 (F)

THE PET FEUD

I LIVED WITH MEGAN for two years in Los Angeles—we're both animal lovers, and I always knew she wanted to get a dog. I was totally supportive of this, and a year into our lease, she got a cute toy poodle from a breeder—very manageable for our 1,200-square-foot apartment. She went home over the holidays to pick up the dog, and two days later, while she was at home with her parents, there was some kind of freak accident with the dog. She was incredibly distraught when he died. It was so, so sad, and I knew she was upset so I tried to give her a bit of space.

Her parents took her to a shelter to look at other dogs to cheer her up, and that's where she found another puppy she liked, which she brought back to our apartment. It was a rescue puppy, and five times the size of her original dog, but I was fine with it. Megan took responsibility for everything, and I was more than willing to play cool aunt to the dog, who she named Ruby. There were a bunch of incidents where Ruby wasn't great, such as when she chewed up my hundred-dollar computer charger. Megan paid me back, and it was okay, because puppies are going to do what puppies do. She bought a massive crate for the dog in the living room, which eventually exploded with toys and other dog stuff. I moved most of my things into my room because I didn't want them to get chewed or peed on.

Ruby did get better, but she was a forty-pound dog in a two-bedroom apartment. I don't think either of us knew how big she was going to get when Megan first adopted her—it went from a toy poodle that would fit in your purse to a dog I couldn't walk because she was so strong. I did love her—I love all animals—but because she was a rescue puppy, she was scared of loud noises. Once she pooped in my room because there was a car crash outside of my apartment and the noise scared her.

A few months went by, and I began to think about getting a cat. I had started working long hours, and was going through an awful breakup. I told Megan that I was thinking about it, and she was very supportive. We went to an adoption day together, where I found a sweet kitten I bonded with immediately. They let me adopt her for a week-long test run, because we weren't sure how she would interact with Ruby.

The great thing about cats is how independent they are. Mine did typical kitten things like sleep a lot, scratch a few things, and chew the plants a little, but I knew I could teach her to grow out of it. I kept her in my room while I was sleeping, but when I went to work, I left my door open so she could have space to run around. Meanwhile, Megan's dog was in the crate in the living room.

I started noticing that when I got home, my kitten was in my bedroom with the door closed. This stressed me out a bit, especially after three days in a row, because my bedroom isn't big enough for a cat to run around in all day. I confronted Megan on the fourth day, and told her it was important for my kitten to be able to run around. Megan never grew up with cats, and it turned out she hates them, so I don't know why she said it was okay for me to get one. She told me, "No, the cat has to stay in your room during the day, because most of the stuff in the living room is mine. Plus, it's not fair for Ruby to be in her crate all day and see a cat running around."

At this point, Megan had already taken over the entire apartment with dog stuff, and I felt like I only lived in my bedroom. Plus, Ruby was peeing everywhere—for the first couple of months, she peed anytime someone came over because she got really excited. The apartment smelled like crap for the first three months with the dog, and I'd bought cleaning stuff and helped her train Ruby, and it surprised me that she did a complete 180 when I got the kitten. It felt really unfair.

When the week ended, I decided to give the kitten back. It was incredibly hard, and I didn't even tell Megan. When she asked me where the kitten was later that day, I told her that I had taken her back because I felt bad that she didn't have room to run around in and had to be alone in my room when I was gone all day. Megan tried to cheer me up by buying me alcohol, but I was sad because I did feel I had bonded with the kitten. The only reason I felt okay about giving her up was because the adoption agency had told me another family was interested in her.

As soon as our lease was up, I moved out. I wanted a one-bedroom, but at the last minute decided to live with a friend from grad school who also loves cats. That was the one condition of me agreeing to live with her. Now I have two cats and I absolutely love them. I only wanted one at first because I was working long hours. But the rescue agency told me that indoor cats tend to do better when there are two so they can play with each other and don't get lonely. These two adorable black cats are brothers—I've named them Bert and Ernie. They're pretty much identical and I have a hard time telling them apart without their collars. They're doing great, and the best part is, my roommate gets along with them really well—she even helps me take care of them from time to time.

—K, 27 (F)

THE ROACH MOTEL

EVA AND I WORK in the same industry, but had never met when she was recommended to me as a potential roommate. Before we started apartment hunting, we scheduled a roommate date to make sure neither of us was crazy. The date went well enough that we're still living together two years later.

The first place we found was described as a "fixer-upper." The price was amazing and the location was great, so we said we'd take it at the open house. We filled out the forms then and there, because three other people were looking at it at the same time. Before we even moved in, we were at the broker's office with the landlady and Eva asked a question about the lease. The landlady turned to her and said, "Why are you so uptight? You don't need to ask about that." And went on a ten-minute rampage about how we needed to live our lives and not worry about lease questions. That should have been a tip-off for us.

Two weeks before we were scheduled to move in, Eva went to take a look at the apartment, and that was the first time we saw a cockroach. The place hadn't been lived in for a month and a half, so we thought it would be okay. The landlady refused to give us her phone number, so the only way we could communicate with her was by slipping notes under her door. After a month or two, she had an exterminator come in, so we figured the situation was taken care of. But the cockroaches kept coming back.

One night, around eleven, I heard Eva scream. A cockroach had climbed up the wall onto her bed, and she had to throw out her bedding and replace everything. I had big closets, and every time I opened them I saw a cockroach chilling there. And I once saw one on my ceiling, which was too high for the roach zapper to reach. I couldn't sleep until it climbed down—the roach was like Rambo, running across ceilings and walls. Boric acid wasn't working, so we started putting down glue sheets and traps everywhere. I put a glue sheet under the radiator and the next morning, there were ten roaches stuck there. I finally snapped when I was heating up dinner in the microwave one night and found a cockroach underneath my Tupperware.

Even the exterminator, a nice guy who returned month after month, couldn't believe we were still having a problem. He told us that we needed to fill in the cracks and holes in the apartment, because the roaches were likely coming from the unit below—where the landlady lived. But she kept insisting that she had lived there for a long time and never seen a single cockroach.

Eva wrote the landlady a polite note saying that the exterminator had recommended that we seal up the holes because the roaches might be coming from underneath. And the next call we got was from our broker, saying that it didn't sound like we were very happy with the living situation, so we should probably move out. This was after about ten months of living there, with exterminators coming once a month. Apparently our demands were too much for the landlady. When we found a new apartment we liked, we were required to put our last landlord down as a reference. I wanted to lie, but Eva is an honest person, so she put her down and of course we didn't get the place.

I don't know how we lived like that for almost a year, but we made it happen. Eva and I bonded over this whole experience.

We had completely opposite schedules and didn't see each other most days, so the cockroach situation made us closer in that we were always chatting online, drafting notes to the landlady, and dealing with apartment issues. There was a frozen yogurt place a few blocks down, and we always went there to vent about the apartment and life in general. In a way, the roaches brought us together. Eva and I used to joke that if there were going to be that many cockroaches in the apartment, they needed to chip in on rent. We certainly didn't need any extra roachmates.

—S, 26 (F)

THE RENT STIFFER

AFTER I GRADUATED FROM COLLEGE, my friends and I found a great place in New York. It was a four-bedroom apartment with a tiny closet space that could be called a fifth room. Even with only a single twin bed and a very small nightstand in there, the door didn't open all the way—it was more like a coffin than a room. Five of us moved in together, and the guy who took the tiniest room was actually living with his girlfriend and needed a place to tell his parents he was staying. When he moved out to get married, it was a significant hit to our rent, so we knew we needed to find a new roommate to take his place.

We posted the opening on a Web site that's like Craigslist for Jewish people—all four of us are Jewish and observe Sabbath and keep a kosher kitchen, which we had to make clear in our post. We said we had a very small room in a nice, huge apartment, and that it's a good place to crash during the week but is tiny. One guy's dad came in to take a look at the room for his son, and he said, "This is fine for Will." We weren't sure if his son needed to take a look at the room, but he said he would show him pictures.

When Will showed up, he was huge—probably around six foot three and three hundred pounds—and the room was maybe only four by eight feet total. Will was not a pleasant person to be around. On his very first night in the apartment, a basketball game was on TV, and we asked if he wanted to watch. "If I wanted to watch black people run and jump and steal, I can go back to my neighborhood," he said. He was a shady guy who worked for his dad and paid his rent in cash every month. He also had a menacing odor that filled the room. He was a very hairy guy who never wore a shirt, and once when we were talking in my room, he leaned back against my window and rubbed his back against it like a giant grizzly bear. That odor is still hanging around my room two years later.

When Will moved out, he owed us the last month's rent and miscellaneous expenses, which came to around $1,500. He left a check with my roommate Aaron, who he'd been paying his share of the rent to, but the check bounced. When we tried to get him to send us another check, that one bounced too. We kept trying to meet up with him, but he always found some excuse not to be there, or showed up at our apartment when we were all asleep.

Will stopped taking our calls and e-mails, and over a year later, we told him, "If you don't pay us back, we're going to take this to small claims court." We gave him a date six months in the future and told Will if he didn't pay us by then we were going to sue him. He knew he owed us the money, and it was enough money that we took measures to try and get it back.

After Will left, we still wanted to fill the room, so we posted it on the Jewish Web site again. This time, we found Sam, a nice guy I'd gone to college with. Sometime between college and that point, he had smoked his brains out, and was not an entirely functioning member of society. He was a huge slob, but he wasn't just messy, he was innovatively messy in that he was always leaving his things in places you could never imagine. It turned into a parlor game of sorts with our friends: Where did Sam leave his things? It was always incredibly random—we found his sneakers in the pantry, chewed gum on the kitchen counter, dirty coffee mugs in the bathroom sink, empty Diet Mountain Dew cans on the bathroom floor, a package of Styrofoam plates in the fridge, and a raw onion in the cabinet where we kept the glassware. When I asked him about the gum, he said, "I'm sorry, I forgot I put it there."

Six months later, Will still hadn't paid us even though he said he would. Aaron, who was studying law, and I went to small claims court, which is an unbelievable experience. We actually had a fun time there. When you arrive, you tell the court whether the claim is being contested or not. If only one side shows up, you move on through to the noncontested process. We met with our lawyer, an older woman, who essentially renders a judgment. We gave her all our documentation, including texts and such, and she looked up at Aaron and said, "Are you in law school?" It turned out she had gone to the same law school as Aaron—we knew from there that we were good. The lawyer put a lien on Will's credit, which means he can't apply for a loan or anything until he pays us back. This was about six months ago, and we still haven't seen the money.

After Sam moved out, the four of us made a unanimous decision to split the cost rather than rent out the room again. We've all come to the realization that the kind of person who is willing to live in that closet-size room is probably someone we don't want to live with.

—M, 28 (M)

THE EX-BOYFRIEND

WHEN I WAS TWENTY-TWO, I moved in with my boyfriend. We'd been dating for about a year when we moved in together, and things went rapidly downhill from there. We only lived together for six months, but it was one of those sad end of the relationship things where we should have broken up earlier but we tried to fix it by moving in together.

Living together was a make or break it kind of situation. I started noticing how much he drank, and all the things that annoyed us slightly about each other suddenly became huge. The smallest things became annoying, like how he pronounced certain words, or his little habits. When you're not living with someone and not around them all the time, you can suck it up. But when you're seeing them constantly, it makes you grit your teeth. We had loads of conversations—this isn't good, how can we make it better, and so on. Living together dragged our breakup out for months, rather than having one "it's over" conversation.

Finally, I couldn't take it anymore, and said I was moving out. I crashed with a bunch of friends who had a spare room in a massive house with six people. They let me live there rent-free for a few weeks, while my boyfriend stayed in our house.

At the time, I worked at a bar, which paid really badly—it was minimum wage, but you were allowed to pay yourself in alcohol while you were working, which is so not legal. There was a tradition at the bar where if you worked on a Friday or Saturday, you took a shot an hour. The bar staff took turns choosing what spirit you took a shot of, and it got messy. People were always trying to outdo each other by picking the most disgusting, old, dusty bottle from the back of the bar. One Friday, about three weeks after the breakup, I was working the most ridiculous shift, which started at six P.M. and finished up at three in the morning. The only good thing about it was that you got a free taxi ride home to be safe when the shift was over. So at three A.M., I was really merry and had had loads of shots. Since this was in the middle of a big breakup, I was drunk and emotional at the same time. I went outside, got in a taxi, and at that stage of the night, had forgotten I moved out of our house, so I gave the driver my old address. It was only when the taxi dropped me off that I realized that my boyfriend and I had broken up and I didn't live there anymore. This was the saddest thing in the world at four in the morning, especially because it was wintertime and freezing. I was at a house that wasn't my house, I didn't have the keys, and I knew he was inside but I couldn't go in.

So I sat in the garden like a creepy person until it got light, and all of the emotion of the breakup and the booze hit home. I sat in the garden and cried and felt sorry for myself until about seven in the morning. And the worst part was, when it was light out and I stood up to leave, I could see in the bedroom window because the curtain was open, and there was a girl there. So not only had I gone and slept in the garden of a house I didn't live in, but I also found out my ex was seeing someone else a few weeks after we broke up. It was the first time I'd ever lived with a boy, and I had all these Disney ideas of how incredible it would be, that we'd play house and it would be amazing. But the reality is, it was doomed from the start.

—B, 29 (F)

THE CRAIGSLIST BEST FRIEND

AFTER LIVING IN TEXAS FOR A FEW YEARS, I decided I wanted to do something crazy and move somewhere far away for a new experience. I started looking for public relations jobs in San Francisco and Boston. A lot of my friends in advertising and PR had headed to New York, but I wasn't looking for jobs there because I was a bit apprehensive about moving to such a big and expensive city.

I applied for a few different jobs, and one Boston company offered me a position in their New York office. The only time I'd been to New York before was when I was eleven, and I hated it because it was so hot in the middle of July—and I'm from Texas.

Once I got the job, they said I could start in three weeks. I had to find a new place to live quickly, even though I didn't know any of the neighborhoods or anyone out there looking for a roommate. I got on Craigslist immediately. In Texas, finding a roommate on Craigslist is really sketchy. It's not like in New York, where it's very normal. If you tell Texans you're doing that, they'll look at you like you're a serial killer. But I was desperate, and I knew other people who had found living situations that way.

I saw a bunch of weird ads on Craigslist before I saw Jamie's. She and her roommate, Kevin, were living in Westchester and wanted to move into Manhattan. They were looking for a third roommate to make it more affordable. I saw a photo of them and thought they looked normal, so I sent them a note.

Meanwhile, Jamie was getting a ton of responses to her post and looking through them at work. Her coworker Matt was helping her go through the replies to weed out the bad ones, and he saw mine. "I think you should pick her," he said. "She seems like the coolest one."

Jamie, Kevin, and I agreed that they'd start looking for a place, and if they hadn't found something by the time I arrived, we'd all look together. I went back on Craigslist to look for an apartment, and I found one on the Upper West Side that looked great and affordable. And it happened that Kevin had seen the same listing and liked it as well. The two of them went to see it and fell in love with it. "We want to take it off the market immediately," they said. "Are you in?" It felt crazy to commit to a lease with people I'd never met before, but I knew I had to go with my instinct, and told them I was in.

I moved to New York a few days later and went to check out the apartment. The landlord was meeting me there so I could sign the lease and hand over a three-thousand-dollar deposit—even though I still hadn't met my future roommates yet. I finally met Jamie later that night for drinks. Since we'd already signed the lease, I had my fingers crossed that we'd actually like each other.

When we met, I hinted that the whole Craigslist thing was pretty scary for me because I hadn't done anything like it before. "Me either," Jamie said. "I told my family you were Kevin's friend of a friend, because I didn't want them to know I was living with a total stranger." That broke the ice a bit between us.

It only took days after we moved in together for Jamie and me to become close. We're around the same age, and we both loved to take long walks and explore the city on the weekend.

When it was nice out, we spent all day lying in Central Park. We were similar in many ways, and we were twenty-three and young and single then, so we went out all the time.

Jamie was constantly telling me about her coworkers, because they were really close. One day about a month after I moved to New York, they had all gone to the beach together and were at an apartment not far from ours, hanging out and drinking, and she told me to come and meet them. That's the first time I met Matt—the guy who told her to pick me as a roommate. I thought he was funny, and definitely my type, but I didn't want to be the annoying girl who hooks up with her friend's coworkers. I hung out with them as a group a few times, and Matt and I made out once or twice but nothing happened beyond that. There were a few times when Jamie hinted that the two of us should date, but I didn't take it seriously.

The next summer, I went to a party at his house, and as Jamie and I were leaving, she told me that she thought Matt liked me. After that night, we started texting, meeting up, and going on dates. It wasn't until we were officially dating that Matt told me the story about how he was actually the one who picked me to live with Jamie.

Kevin moved out of our apartment six months later to move in with his girlfriend, but Jamie and I stayed for three more years. The first person to take over Kevin's room was an acquaintance from college. She only lived with us for six months but was completely insane—she did a lot of drugs, brought guys home all the time, and was always having ridiculously loud sex. The second girl, who I found through my college's alumni Web site, was cool but had her own stuff going on. It was apparent within a few months that she wanted to keep her distance, which was fine with us. We didn't form that deep of a connection with her—it was never on the same level Jamie and I had.

At one point, we found a rat in our apartment, and it was the most traumatizing thing I've ever been through. I plugged my door with towels so it couldn't get into my bedroom, but it was in our apartment for a week. The exterminator came and put poison around our kitchen, and Jamie came home one day and smelled it under the sink. She had to fish the rat out after it had eaten the poison and died. It was the bravest thing ever.

After we lived together for four years, Jamie recently moved out of the city. I miss her already. I owe everything to her—my first apartment, my first friend in New York, and of course, my boyfriend—who is now my new roommate.

—E, 27 (F)

THE BUSINESS PARTNERS

ON MY FIRST DAY OF COLLEGE AT GEORGETOWN, I met Nicolas Jammet, who lived next door to me in the dorms. We lived in Harbin Hall, which is famous because it's where Bill Clinton lived—his room was actually on our floor. Nic's family is in the food business—they used to own La Caravelle in New York, which closed our freshman year. The two of us built a friendship off of our love for food. Once a month or so, in order to escape the terrible cafeteria food, we explored the city and found new restaurants. I also met Nathaniel Ru very early on freshman year. We were in the same Accounting 101 class, and became friends because we're both from Los Angeles and bonded over that. The two of us love music and went to a lot of concerts together.

It wasn't until junior year of college that Nate and I moved into an on-campus apartment together. Nic took over our apartment when the two of us went abroad, and when we moved back, the three of us stayed neighbors. During our senior year, Nate and I lived together in an apartment on Bank Street, and Nic lived around the corner. Our apartment became our first office and the place where we came up with our company. The idea for Sweetgreen, a salad restaurant with fast, healthy food, came about because we had a need for it. We wanted to eat healthily in a simple, affordable, hip way. The girls around us have inspired a lot of our best ideas—one of our girlfriends complained about not having great food in the area, and we felt the same way. So we found an incredible location on our street, which was only 550 square feet, for our first Sweetgreen store. The small space forced us to keep the concept boiled down: a seasonal kitchen selling salads, cold-pressed juices, and rice bowls, with ingredients from local farms. We might have been tempted to add sandwiches or other things early on, but we didn't have the space.

The first store opened the summer after we graduated. All three of us were studying business, and we wrote a business plan, raised money, and built the store while we were still in school. We knew there was a need for a restaurant like Sweetgreen, so we were confident in the first store, but we didn't realize how big it could be. We wanted to create a brand—the idea of a lifestyle we wanted to live and a brand we believed in really excited us. But I don't think we ever thought that we'd have eighteen restaurants in the greater D.C. area alone, plus one in New York, one in Boston, and two in Philadelphia.

Becoming business partners has made us much closer. It's a never-ending conversation we have. Our idea of the sweet life is where work and play are intertwined, and that is absolutely our life. We work all the time, but it doesn't feel like we're working, and that's why we're successful. It's fun, and we're doing it with people we truly love. We've learned to disagree and not let it affect our relationship. Usually the three of us can come to a consensus on big decisions, but when one person disagrees, we're still able to go get dinner, have a drink, and move on.

Nate and I have lived together ever since, and Nic has always lived very close by. A few years ago, Nate and I bought a house from our entrepreneurship professor—who also happens to be one of our investors and mentors. And Nic and his twin brother bought a condo across the street, which I have the code to, so it's almost like we live with Nic too.

We no longer work out of our apartment. We now have an office in D.C.'s Chinatown with ten or so employees. It's a cool, creative space with an open floor plan and exposed brick that we call the Treehouse. We joke that we should probably have beds there, because we're there more than we are at home.

Since we opened our New York store, we've been splitting our time between D.C. and New York, and the three of us also share an apartment in New York. We spend so much time together that we've developed an ESP of sorts—sometimes we'll go to work separately and show up wearing the same outfit.

I do think about how lucky we are to have met one another—it's all very *Sliding Doors*. The three of us really value one another's friendship and opinions. We did a TED Talk last year on the idea of partnerships. If I told you Sweetgreen was a salad shop, you'd say, "Okay, cool." But it's much more than that—it's a lifestyle that we want to live and share with other people. When you're starting a company, it's not about what you do, but why you do it and who you do it with.

—JONATHAN NEMAN, 29 (M),
COFOUNDER AND CEO OF SWEETGREEN

YOUNG AT HEART

THE THREE-MONTH RV TRIP

WHILE I WAS LIVING IN LOS ANGELES, a childhood friend of mine, Beth, and her boyfriend, Pete, contacted me about a company they'd founded. The two of them had started teaching specialty fitness classes in New York, and were receiving a lot of interest from LA. They flew to the West Coast a few times for work and stayed with me, and eventually decided to bring me on as a brand ambassador.

I got more and more involved with the company by helping out at events and being an extra set of hands, and I officially joined when I moved back east during the summer. That spring, Beth and Pete had applied to be on *Shark Tank*, the reality TV show for start-up funding. After they were accepted onto the show, they went back to Los Angeles once more to film a fourteen-minute segment. You essentially have to pitch a bunch of "shark" investors and give them all the financial information about your company. Every single one of the investors made them an offer, which is rare. They accepted a six-figure offer from Mark Cuban, the billionaire owner of the Dallas Mavericks, for 30 percent of the company.

Mark encouraged us to think outside the box in terms of how to capitalize on the publicity of the show and reach people across the country, and that's partially how we came up with the idea of the three-month road trip. There were four of us involved at the time: Pete, the CEO; Beth, the head trainer who developed the fitness program; Rick, who did operations and shipping; and me, handling marketing and the logistics of the tour. We decided to go on tour from mid-October to January and drive around the country in an RV with all our fitness equipment to teach classes, host trainer certifications at various gyms, and build brand awareness.

Our thirty-foot RV seemed like a good size, but those RVs are built for families with two or three kids under the age of ten. When you have three guys over six feet, it's much less comfortable. We knew immediately that if we stayed in hotels every night, the costs would add up quickly. We all agreed to sleep in the RV during the trip, but there was only one full-size bed in it, which Beth and Pete shared. Rick took a five-foot-long couch, and I slept on a table that turned into a bench. Every night for three months, I curled up and slept on my side, because I was too tall for the bench. I actually developed lockjaw on the left side of my face. Beth and Pete also insisted on bringing their nine-month-old bulldog—a loud snorer—on the trip. It was a test not only of business relationships but of personal ones as well.

The trip started in Connecticut, and we were supposed to have a huge kickoff party in New York at Chelsea Piers, a nice gym off a park on the west side. We had celebrities scheduled to come, and then Hurricane Sandy hit. All our stops in the upper East Coast area had to be postponed or canceled. It was a rough start to our three-month tour.

We continued along our way, stopping at gyms every day, teaching classes, and trying to run our company from the RV at the same time. We were never in the same place for more than forty-eight hours, and someone had to be driving at all times. When we did park it was either next to a highway or on a busy lit street. If we slept for three hours, it was a good night. Five hours and we were feeling like royalty. We'd decided early on that we wouldn't be using the RV's bathroom, because if we did, we'd have to empty the sewage at an RV park. We figured we'd save money and time if we used the facilities at gyms and restaurants. It proved how strong our bladders could be. We spent many nights in Home Depot or Walmart parking lots, bringing our Dopp kits to the bathrooms to wash our faces, splash water under our arms, brush our teeth, and floss, while employees and customers came in and out.

The trip took us down the East Coast, and for one of our legs, we had to drive through the night from Atlanta to Miami. I was driving through a random part of north Florida at three thirty in the morning when all of a sudden there was a massive explosion on the left side of the RV. It lifted the whole left side up and slammed it down, which woke everyone up. They thought I had hit something, but actually both tires on the left back side were rotted and had exploded simultaneously. We had to call Triple A and slowly drive our vehicle to the next exit so a guy could change the tires. We didn't get back on the road until seven or eight, and by then I was exhausted and asked someone else to drive.

Pete picked up the driving, and all the guys were upset with me because they thought I hit something. And that's when the exact same thing happened on the right side. Now we had four exploded tires, and no chance of making the television appearance and launch party we had scheduled in Miami.

Later, while we were driving through Texas to the West Coast, we found out there were mice in the RV. We saw droppings everywhere, and Beth saw them in the bedroom from time to time. The dealer we'd rented from said that it was possible that mice could have come in from outside, and offered to get us an exterminator, but there wasn't much we could do.

The only good thing was that the stops themselves were going well—we were getting great responses from the trainers, which was keeping us afloat, because everything else on the trip was backfiring. We were looking forward to getting to the warm weather on the West Coast, but when we got to San Diego, we were exhausted and miserable. We were in the gym by six in the morning and staying until the evening, so we barely even saw daylight.

In LA, we were scheduled to do a *Shark Tank* follow-up with Mark Cuban. We had to pull ourselves together even though we looked like crap and hadn't slept at all. They wanted to film the RV but there was no way we could show the inside, with blankets and dog food and toys everywhere.

We drove north to Seattle, and were heading southeast through Colorado when we hit an incredibly bad storm. The blizzard was so strong that we could only go four miles an hour in the RV, and we were scared there wouldn't be enough gas to make it through. We kept canceling stops in between because we couldn't make it in time.

Indianapolis was the saving grace of the tour, socially speaking. One of the gyms we were working with was the official gym of the Colts cheerleaders. We were finally able to do our first official launch party there, with thirty cheerleaders and an Indy race car driver. Rick and I, the single guys, went out for the first time on the trip to try and have fun.

By late December, we were getting close to the end of the tour. We had gone the whole trip without any more major incidents and were back in Boston when Beth pulled into a street parking spot. That's when she hit a car with the RV's stepladder. This would have been fine, except the stepladder got stuck and caught the bumper of the car and ripped it out entirely. That's when we knew for sure we weren't getting our security deposit back. Plus, the inside was trashed—the couch was ripped up, the floor was filthy, there was dog hair everywhere.

Our plan was to go home to New Hampshire, where we'd look for an actual office and living space to share. But after sleeping within ten feet of one another for months, everyone was thinking the same thing: if we lived together, we'd probably kill each other.

The tour itself was a success in terms of what we'd set out to achieve. Before the tour we were only working with two gyms, and afterward we had seventy-five locations signed on and had certified more than five hundred trainers. Fitness is very trend-based, and we were part of the new craze. The four of us became very close, and I think that contributed to our success, but living and working together was also incredibly frustrating, and ultimately, that's why I left.

It was cool to travel the country, meet people, and see the success of a company in real time. Living in an RV for months is something I can now check off my list. I haven't been in an RV since. If anyone wants to go camping, I'll have to think long and hard before I do it again.

—N, 26 (M)

THE JERSEY SHORE HOUSE

TWO SUMMERS AGO, after years of hassling, I finally decided to join my friends at their twenty-person Jersey Shore house. The house has been passed down via friends through the years, and we're very close with the landlord's family. There's a real estate agent involved, but it's a formality. Until the day we tell the landlord we don't want the house for the summer, it'll always stay ours. The house has two floors, with five bedrooms, eleven beds, a living room, a kitchen, three bathrooms—one is designated just for dudes, the others are unisex—and an outdoor shower. There's a patio with a barbecue grill and canopy and kiddie pool. There's always beer pong going on or something on the grill—it's a relaxed environment. Some people rage all day long, but we're a bit older and more chill.

People have bad impressions of the Jersey Shore because of the damn show, but it's nothing like that. Some think that shore houses are full of deadbeats, but we're actually all pretty legitimate human beings. The average age is thirty-three, and we have two lawyers, a hedge-fund guy, and financial advisors. Everyone has real jobs. It's not just a bunch of guidos—there are actually only two or three Italians in the house. There are a few similarities to the show—there's definitely drama—but nothing that serious. I've never seen anyone get into a fight.

This past summer, only five of us came back, so we had a fifteen-person turnover. We struggled a bit with finding housemates, because you have to sign people up as early as March. I recruited a few people from college, so we had about ten people committed before we put our Craigslist ad out, which filled the rest of the spots. We interview everyone before we take their money—we don't want crazy psycho people. The commitment is from Memorial Day to Labor Day. The full share is $2,000 for the summer and $1,500 for a half share, which covers rent, utilities, the party fund, and a cleaning lady. Some homes operate with half shares that have alternating schedules so that lots of people can come down, but with our house, you can come down whenever. The only reason we have full shares and half shares is because full shares have their own space, with a bed and dresser. Half shares aren't guaranteed that kind of space when they come down. If a full-share bed is open while they're here, they have dibs on it. But if not, they sleep on one of five or six couches.

Every member of the house can come whenever they want. Our rule is that guests have to bring a thirty-pack or a bottle of liquor to the house. Some houses charge guests, but we're very relaxed. You can bring as many guests as you want; some will bring two or three people. I rarely bring people down—I don't like mixing my worlds. The house can get really full, with people sleeping on the floor without blankets or pillows, or on deflated air mattresses.

Everyone shares rooms at the house. Two years ago, I shared a room with this girl Erica, who I had just met. On the very first weekend, over Memorial Day, she hooked up with my best guy friend, Tim. No one knew they were secretly hooking up for about a month or so. I spent hours and hours on the phone with him every night, talking it out. Fast-forward a year later, and they're now moving in together. You don't get to choose who you bunk up with, but Tim thought Erica and I would be a good fit. I met her at the house, and she's one of my best friends now.

My role in the house is being everyone's friend. Everyone tells me everything, I hang out with everyone, and I don't like to cause drama. I go down to the shore house to have a good time. There's a girl in our house who on the very first weekend of the summer started hooking up with—but not sleeping with—one of the guys in the house. While that was fizzling out, she told me drunkenly that she hooked up with another male housemate back at home in Hoboken. Basically, she started liking him, and he didn't like her back—it was all very high school, and they often had late-night drunken arguments. It got really drawn out, and he wanted nothing to do with her. On the Fourth of July, he brought two girls back to the house and walked in right in front of her. She had a conniption and stormed out of the house. People tend to avoid going down on the same weekend after they've hooked up.

This past summer, I lived with Amy, a thirty-one-year-old divorcée from New York. She decided to do the shore house to meet new friends. I got a weird vibe from her from day one—she is a skinny, pretty woman and I could tell she liked to be the center of attention in front of guys. I didn't think I would like her.

The summer before, I'd been hooking up with the landlord's son. I was twenty-nine and he was twenty-five—he's a cute all-American boy. It wasn't anything serious, and we even went skiing together in the winter. But I told myself I wasn't going to get involved again this year, because it was too much pressure. On Saturday of Memorial Day weekend, I saw the landlord's son and my roommate Amy, the divorcée, at a bar, and I knew the two of them were going to hook up.

Two days later, on Monday, I went to our room and the door was closed. I knocked, and she said, "Just a minute!" I could hear clothes and a guy's voice. Three minutes later Amy opened the doors, and they were both in there. I turned white as a ghost. They hooked up all summer, and I kept walking in on them because she didn't lock the door. It could have been weird, but it wasn't because I'm not interested in him anymore—mainly because I started seeing someone else at the shore house. My guy is thirty-eight, and he's been divorced for a year and a half, because his wife cheated on him with a guy who was at their wedding.

One Sunday morning, I was in bed with my guy, and the landlord's son came in and climbed into bed with Amy. The four of us were pillow talking for over an hour. In my head, I was like, *What has my life come to?* We were sitting there gabbing like two couples.

I broke my no-house-hookup rule this summer, but there's no drama with us. We actually like each other, and it's fun. I generally don't hook up with housemates because nine times out of ten it turns into a disaster. But what's interesting is that a lot of romance stems from the house. Off the top of my head right now, I can think of five couples who met at the house who are engaged or married. I'm going to a wedding in two weeks, a couple got engaged in February, and a couple weekends ago, two separate sets of couples who met at the house got engaged. My friends Tim and Erica are moving in together, and there's no doubt in my mind they'll eventually get married. They say you can't find love on the Jersey Shore, but I know many who have.

—K, 30 (F)

THE ROOMANCE

WHEN I FIRST MOVED into a shared house in Toronto, I arrived a day before all of my other roommates. I moved from across the country into an empty room without furniture and slept on the floor on a pile of my clothes. I felt incredibly sorry for myself, because I had no friends yet and didn't know what my three roommates looked like or what kind of people they were—I'd met them all online through my brother.

The next day, Liz showed up with a U-Haul and her boyfriend. I tried to help her move in, but felt out of place because they were older than me. That's when Greg, another roommate, came in the door. And I kid you not, it was love at first sight. I couldn't stop staring at him—he looks like James Dean and is not hard to look at. He had a way of breezing into a room and charming people by being mysterious and interesting. We lived together for two years, and I always felt like I wore my affection on my sleeve a little too much. He had a girlfriend, so I never put myself out there or made it obvious. And he was older than me by five years, which felt like a big gap at the time.

My pile of clothes eventually turned into a mattress on the floor, and that's how I lived for two years. Greg, on the other hand, had a nice adult room with furniture. The wall that we shared was actually quite thin, and sometimes when I was getting something out of my closet, I could hear him doing the same thing, and it gave me a weird sense of excitement knowing he was on the other side of the wall. I adored him from the beginning. It was as if he could do nothing wrong. I'm the youngest in my family and have always felt like I'm not taken seriously around older people. I felt like he thought of me as a silly little girl. I used to run to the bathroom in my underwear and a tank top, or fly around the house in a whirlwind. I was the girl with three jobs and not a care in the world. There were a few instances while we were living together where I got a glimpse that the crush was maybe mutual. But Greg is very good at holding his cards close to his chest, and it was never enough for me to tell him that I liked him and see what happened.

Once, we were in the backyard waiting for the friends he had invited over for a barbecue. For some reason, people weren't showing up, and he had bought a bunch of beer and food. It was the two of us sitting around, me pretending to read my book and he probably doing the same. We never shared a lot of words or developed a good rapport.

It was a beautiful day out, and after a long silence, he looked over and said, "Why don't you go put on a sundress?" I've never been spoken to like that before. It was one of those things that makes your stomach do backflips and gets you all hot and bothered. The way he said such a simple thing was really sexy. The book went flying out of my hand, and I ran upstairs and tried on four or five dresses, and came down after settling on a yellow one. But at the same time I was running downstairs to make my little debut, a bunch of his friends showed up, and the moment was lost.

We had these little moments over and over again. Once we were both hungover and spent Saturday morning in the living room, passed out on two couches that formed an L-shape. Our heads were close, and he took out his guitar and played some of his favorite songs for me—it was very intimate.

While in Toronto, I was traveling quite a bit for work—I was gone for a few months at a time on assignments. I remember missing home, and he once wrote me an e-mail out of the blue. When I got home, my roommates teased me about how he had brought me up in conversation several times over the past few months. I kept getting excited that maybe he liked me, but there was no indication from him that he ever did.

Eventually, he was accepted into school in Los Angeles and moved there with his girlfriend, who was a stern older woman. She was a decade older than me, so that was another weird factor. The day before he left, he mentioned that he was having good-bye drinks at a bar and that we should stop by. I was working three jobs back-to-back in a single day at the time, and when I got to the bar, everyone was gone. I went home thinking I'd run into him there and he'd be drunk and maybe I'd finally tell him how I felt before he left. But I got home and nobody was there and it was a big empty house again, because everyone had started moving their things out. That's when it began to set in that this nice little phase of my life was over. I got bold and texted him that I wished I'd had the chance to say good-bye, and he responded with something stoic and nondescript, like "Oh, too bad." He's a man of few words. And that's where I tipped my hand and said, "Probably better this way."

Sure enough, he went to Los Angeles and I didn't hear from him for months. It was about six months later when I found out from Liz that he had broken up with his girlfriend. And in the same year, Liz got engaged to the same boyfriend who had helped her move in.

I was single, still living in Toronto, and going through a series of nonrelationships. I had dated some people, but it never clicked. Then Liz's wedding came around, and I sent Greg an e-mail to ask if he was going. He wrote back that he wasn't sure of his schedule. I have a tendency to be jokingly bossy, and I told him he had to come because we owed it to Liz, who had brought us all together, and that it would be fun. And he wrote back, "Okay." Which you can interpret in a hundred different ways—that was always my struggle with him, that it was impossible to glean any subtext.

We made a plan to go to the wedding together, and the format was that you could either stay at a bed-and-breakfast or at a campsite. I come from a family of campers but have never attempted to go camping myself. I had it in my head that it would be so romantic if the two of us camped out together. I wasn't thinking of ambushing him with romance, just that it would be nice and quaint and Canadian if we camped together. I asked if he was getting a room or if he wanted to crash in my tent with me—which was a total lie, I didn't even own a tent. I'd never actually camped before, but I made it sound like I did it all the time. He said he'd stay with me because it was cheaper. So I went to a camping equipment store and bought a tent and the nicest sleeping bags you can get. I was so excited and finally making money at my job, so I went all out with my camping gear. When I showed up, I looked like a pro.

We'd also decided to rent a car, but I didn't have my license so he was the one driving. We made a plan to meet at the Montreal airport, and I showed up an hour or so early. I'd recently gotten back from a two-week sailing trip, and had a great tan, really blond hair, glowing skin, and was feeling very good about life in general. He came through the double doors in the arrival area, we looked at each other, and neither of us knew that the other was single at this point, but I was assuming so and so was he. He gave me this huge, whole-body hug, and then ran to the car rental counter to start dealing with things. And I popped in my iPod and started listening to Arcade Fire. I was trying to be cool, even though I was hot and bothered.

We were spending the first night in Montreal at our fourth roommate Karen's place, and assumed she had a guest room. But she just had a twin-size futon that would have only fit a child. It was long enough to lie down on but not even comfortable enough for one person to sleep on. Greg made a hilarious attempt to get comfortable in the armchair, and indicated that he would sleep with his head cocked to the side. I told him we could share the futon, and we wound up very carefully lying next to each other on this twin-size futon without touching each other. We were acting like teenagers who had been forbidden from any sexual contact. Karen had an adorable cat with little mutated mitts—six fingers on each paw. The cat, who had loved to cuddle with me back in Toronto, jumped on the bed and started stepping over us and remembering us. We were both petting the cat because it was between us, and our hands touched. Then the cat jumped off, and we started awkwardly telling each other stories because we were both a bit too wired to go to sleep. The cat then jumped up on the other side of me and pressed itself against my side, sprawling out and taking up space. So that forced me to move a little closer, and at this point, Greg and I realized we only had four hours to sleep before we had to get up and go. We fell asleep nose-to-nose, forehead-to-forehead, and every four minutes or so we both moved a millimeter in the same direction, so by the time we woke up, his arm had curved around my head and was holding me in a nice way. I woke up before him and peeled myself out of bed. I felt like it was the most intimate sleep I'd ever had, and there was something very familiar about it but also very respectful.

On the drive up to the wedding, we had a friend's mom with us who needed a ride. I had hoped it would be just the two of us and that it would be an opportunity to find out what happened with the ex-girlfriend, but the fifty-five-year-old social worker in the backseat kept telling us stories about her work and her drum circle. She was lovely, but the whole time I was looking at him for some sign that what had happened to me last night had also happened to him.

When we arrived at the wedding, things were bustling and we had to change quickly. I'd actually brought the same yellow sundress that I wore in the backyard the time he told me to put on a dress, and I wasn't sure if he would remember. We were in the social worker's bed-and-breakfast room, and this woman was very liberal, whipping her clothes off and standing around naked. I was trying to be discreet, but in my mind, I was thinking, *Great, the first time he sees me with my shirt off is in the context of rapidly changing for a wedding with a middle-aged woman in the room with her breasts hanging out*—not exactly romantic.

We got separated for a bit at the wedding, and I immediately felt a punch in my gut, like I'd lost him and I'd be socializing on my own all night instead of as a couple. It was also uncomfortably hot during the wedding, and I remember thinking, *This isn't attractive. I'm red in the face, and I'm sweating.* It wasn't the perfect setting I'd envisioned where I'd be in a yellow sundress and we'd be together at a wedding in a little country town.

After the wedding ceremony, people went off to do different activities, and a bunch of guests went to the lake to swim. I wanted to go but couldn't find Greg, so I decided to set up the tent, because I realized that I hadn't gotten rid of some of the packaging, and I didn't want him to see that it was all new gear. I was unpacking when he came over to help me. Most of the camping spaces were gone so we pitched our tent on a slope. He wanted to go swimming, but I was feeling a bit too shy and spent the rest of the afternoon kicking myself for not being carefree and showing how adventurous I was.

During the reception at night, he was by my side again, noticeably paying attention in a way he wasn't earlier. We got food together, and he referred to the desserts as "events," and said, "Are you going to have some of these little events?" I thought it was so adorable, and was falling in love with him all over again. After the speeches, we started dancing, and this was when it happened. He grabbed my hand and we went to the dance floor; it was a beautiful outdoors pavilion setting, and he didn't let me sit down all night. We spent the next two hours spinning each other around and slow dancing. I didn't see another person all night and neither did he. People started to notice and ask what was happening between the two of us, and I couldn't say anything because in the three years since we'd first met, I'd never felt affection from him.

At one point I got cold, so I decided to go to the tent to get a sweater. He said he'd walk back with me, in case there were bears—a real concern in Quebec. We climbed inside our little tent, and the model happened to be called the Hubba Hubba. Back inside the tent, he lay down and I was making small talk, thinking we would head back to the party, when he leaned over and gave me a peck on the lips. I was not about to settle for a peck after three years of sexual tension, so I grabbed his face and we started kissing. It was the most amazing thing—all these moments where I had hoped and prayed that he liked me back washed through my head. I felt that I had almost willed this to happen after wanting it for so long. We didn't actually have sex, just kissed and went back to the party, but I felt like I'd had a night of sex. Something about the intensity of that kiss was enough—he could have gone off to war for four years and I could have lived off that kiss.

After this amazing night, we woke up the next morning and had both slid to one side of the tent. We were in a heap on a pile of stuff and it was really hot again—not a romantic way to wake up. We were saying our good-byes when Liz, the bride, came over and said, "You guys! I knew it! When are you getting married?" That's when he shared his side of the story: apparently he had liked me all these years, and was always fighting with his own better judgment because he had a girlfriend and was a very loyal person. He had made it known to people that he liked me and had tried to make it known to me subtly—I just hadn't picked up on it. We had a rushed good-bye—we were late for our flights, and from there we kept chatting over texts.

Two weeks later, he came down to visit me in Toronto. He had been saving miles for a decade and blew them all the following year visiting me every two weeks. We didn't go more than three weeks without seeing each other and managed to pull off a long-distance relationship for a year. As he was finishing up school, I was accepted to graduate school in New York, and we decided, though we had never lived in the same city as a couple and had no idea what that would look or feel like, that we were going to move to New York and live together. We went from two people visiting each other and Skyping to moving in together and becoming roommates again in a completely new context.

The journey of retracing these moments that led up to the wedding has been amazing, and I realized that our love story actually started way before that. For me, it started the second I first saw him, and I guess it did for him too. When we first lived together in Toronto, I always cooked and left food out in hopes that people liked it.

I made these elaborate desserts, and my ulterior motive was for my food to be the way to his heart. I cooked huge dinners and baked cheesecakes and hazelnut chocolate cakes, and every time I gave him something to sample, he shrugged and said it wasn't his thing. He never, ever liked my food. I felt like if I couldn't make him love me through my food then there was no hope, because cooking was the one thing I was really good at. When we finally got together and I told him that my cooking was a point of insecurity for me, he told me that he was nuts about my food, but had felt that admitting so would be a betrayal to his girlfriend. Now that it's the two of us living together, he gobbles up my food. It turns out he loves my food and he loves me.

—C, 28 (F)

THE SHOWER INTRUDER

AFTER WORKING ON THE EAST COAST for a few years, I decided to go on a cross-country journey with my friend Jonah. We drove west to California, crashing with friends along the way. In the final leg of the trip, Jonah was staying with his mom in the Bay Area while I stayed with my friend Kat. I'd met Kat's roommate, Leo, before, because he had visited New York and slept on my couch. I didn't know much about him, only that he was an artist who thought he was the cutest guy ever.

I had already been staying at Kat's for a couple of days when I went jogging one morning. I came back and saw Leo cleaning the bathroom, so I asked if he minded if I took a quick shower. I went into the bathroom, but the door wouldn't close because they had towel hooks hanging from it. I figured it wasn't a big deal and went in.

I was shampooing my hair when I thought I saw a shadow on the other side of the shower curtain. I turned and looked out the front to see if the door had opened, but didn't notice anything. When I turned back around, Leo was in the shower with me. He had not only slid past the curtain and into the shower, but had also already sudsed up. "What the hell?" I screamed. "Someone is getting out right now." I thought about hitting him, but we were the only ones home, and I thought the consequences could be much worse if I hit him as opposed to yelling at the top of my lungs. I felt incredibly vulnerable and violated. Leo was quite large and muscular, and the thought of what could have happened was too scary.

"Okay," he said. "I just have to rinse first." He slithered past me, rinsed off, and left. I then rinsed off quickly and ran into Kat's room to call Jonah and have him pick me up. I hurriedly packed up and was waiting on the corner for Jonah when Leo came out to apologize. "I'm so sorry," he said. "I know what I did was stupid and immature, but I wanted you to know that you have a beautiful body." *Yeah*, I thought to myself, *a body that you had no business seeing.*

After Jonah picked me up, we went to see Kat at her job to tell her what had happened. Not only did she kick him out, but he also lost both of his girlfriends—it turned out he had been dating two girls at the same time. The whole Bay Area heard the shower story, and his player actions were exposed—no one else wanted to date him after they found out what a slimeball he was.

—L, 30 (F)

THE NAKED NANNA

I ONCE LIVED IN AN ARTIST-HOUSING BUILDING that was co-run by a nonprofit arts organization and homeless prevention coalition. In order to live there, you had to qualify as an entertainment professional—meaning you've worked in the industry a certain amount in the past two years—and meet an income requirement. There were thirty-some floors in the building—probably close to three hundred people total, with a penthouse floor that housed older former artists with severe nursing needs. It was such an affordable housing option that the wait list was a year long, and when accepted, you were put in wherever there was an open bed. At the time, I only had three weeks to find a place, so a social worker suggested I put a notice on the bulletin board saying I was willing to sublet a room within the building. Sure enough, I got a call from Paula, who said she was going to Los Angeles for two years and needed a subletter.

It was a cool environment—there were a bunch of older people, but for the most part, it was like a music conservatory dorm, with all the requisite drama. One great indication of the insanity of the building was that there was a naked clause on Halloween. They actually put a sign on the elevator saying, "Please wear clothing on Halloween." There was also a rule saying you couldn't make out or have sex in the elevators. When the building first opened, it was almost all gay men, and I guess there was a lot of sex everywhere, so eventually that became a rule.

You could always hear people rehearsing for jobs—once someone upstairs was auditioning for a project that I was working on. We didn't end up hiring him, but it was still cool. Everyone was incredibly nice—when I was trying to get a room, the people in the building helped me in any way they could. Since everyone was an artist, they tended to be open. It was very comfortable to not have to try and be normal. The only downside was that you had a roommate. There were only ten studio units in the building, and of course people moved into those and didn't leave for the rest of their lives.

Before I moved in, Paula had warned me that the first person she was supposed to sublet to had had problems with her roommate. That should have been a red flag, but I needed a place to live and it was such a fantastic location and building that I didn't care who I lived with. I spent twenty hours a day out at work and rehearsal, so I wasn't home very much. "My roommate's older," said Paula. "She's a little difficult and throws little temper tantrums if she's not getting enough attention." I was willing to deal with anything, but I didn't realize the extent of it until I got there.

Paula's roommate was a seventy-five-year-old former actress we called Nanna. The two of them had split the living room down the middle, and Nanna tried to take over the entire living room because she had more stuff—she felt it was her apartment and someone else was living in it. Her side had tons of furniture and stuff crammed into it, while mine had two folding chairs and a cocktail table. There were a lot of boxes after I moved in, and she even called building management because she thought my stuff was taking up too much space in the living room. She started randomly chaining the door so I couldn't come in and out, and I had to tell her, "I paid for this apartment, so I can come in and out when I want." She wanted me to tell her where I was at all times and when I'd be coming back.

About two weeks after I moved in, I was in the living room, where we had a stackable washer-dryer unit next to the kitchen. When I walked in I saw her standing there in nothing but pantyhose and a button-down shirt. I figured she was getting dressed and needed to get something out of the laundry, so I let it go. I'll give anyone the benefit of the doubt once or twice. Except the seminakedness didn't stop. I spotted her going to the trash chute in the hallway in nothing but stockings and a shirt, or sometimes, socks and a shirt. Since she was older, I didn't want to cause any problems. I wasn't home very much anyway.

Then came the day when I walked into the kitchen and she was bent over getting dishes out of the dishwasher with absolutely nothing on. I saw everything. I immediately walked back into my room and closed the door—I didn't know what to do. The weird thing was, she never apologized or looked ashamed or embarrassed. She kept walking around in just a shirt, which was sometimes buttoned and sometimes completely open. Sometimes she wore stockings if I was lucky, otherwise absolutely no underwear. I saw her breasts so many times. And she acted like I was rude for invading her space by constantly giving me looks and sighing at me. We had two bathrooms, and hers was in her room and mine was in the hallway, so it wasn't as if she had to run to and from the shower. She was always hanging out in her part of the living room or in the kitchen, doing normal things people usually wore clothes to do, but in varying degrees of nakedness.

Nanna also got annoyed when I had friends over. Most of my friends are guys, and I was always afraid that they were going to think I was inviting them over so they could get an eyeful of seventy-five-year-old ass. I started warning people who came over, telling them about my naked Nanna situation. "Just be ready and avert your eyes until you're sure she's wearing clothes," I said.

I never confronted her about the nakedness, but I did confront her about other things. She often made a hot mess in the kitchen and didn't clean up. I always made my requests in a polite way, such as "Someone might be coming by, so maybe we should clean up." She did have a few friends come over once in a while, and they hung out in the living room fully dressed. I was almost afraid that one day she would start commenting on the presence of my clothing—I wasn't sure if it was a nudist apartment and Paula had neglected to tell me.

Aside from Nanna, the building was great. The boys next door to me had a shower that was right next to mine, and they were actors or singers who belted show tunes every morning. When I was in my bathroom or shower, I often heard *Wicked* or *Phantom of the Opera* coming through the wall. And you can bet that if it was something I knew, I sang right along with them. I could hear them pause slightly, and then jump right back into it. We never hung out, we only sang together. It was fantastic.

Thanks to the nonprofit arts organization, there were always free tickets to shows, community events, and cool performances from people who lived in the building. A lot of the older actors went to these events and told stories about working in the industry. We had a party to watch the Tonys in the community room, and one older man had a story about every single person who came on the screen. It was so entertaining.

And our security guards knew us better than anyone. When I was sick they checked in on me and did errands for me once in a while. Once I went on a date with a guy at a bar across the street, and he was bad news. He kept saying, "I know where you live and I'm going to come visit sometime"—I guess he thought it was a cute thing to say. I told the girl at the front desk about it, and sure enough, she saw him standing outside our building a few days later. She glared at him and pretended she was getting a weapon—which of course she didn't have—and left a note saying not to let him in. And we were supposed to pay the maintenance guys if we wanted anything special done, but they not only fixed things without pay but also didn't tell management. They were super cool.

I was so happy I got into the building, which I found out about through a guy I call the housing fairy. During the day, I worked at a corporate firm in a huge building. There was a plaza for the whole building where you could eat your lunch on a nice day. I was out there in the spring, and knew I had to move out of my current apartment by the end of summer. I was vaguely thinking about housing but not doing much about it yet. I was sharing a table with a guy who was a visual artist with a day job in the building. He suggested I apply to the artist-housing building he used to live in, but the application was so involved that I waited until I did need housing to actually apply. When I was asked how I'd found out about the building, I told management about the guy who worked at the same building as me. They looked him up and said, "No one by that name has ever lived here." I figured he might have been subletting, so I tried to look him up through our building corporate directory, but his name was nowhere to be found. He'd given me his card, but I lost it. I never found anyone in the building who had ever heard of him, so I'm convinced he was a fairy who came down from heaven to tell me where to live.

—F, 30 (F)

THE STAGED ROBBERY

WHEN I FIRST MOVED to Los Angeles, I stayed with my best friend and his fiancée for two weeks, until that ran its course and I decided to leave. I do stand-up comedy on the side, and the next place I moved to was a house with seven other comedians. It was actually sad. You might think comedians are hilarious and joking all the time, but it's actually morose and bad. The opposite of what happens on the stage happens at home. We were all wondering, *Am I going to make it? Am I doing the right thing?* I lived there for three months, sharing a bathroom with four people, two of whom I never met the whole time I was staying there—it was basically a public restroom.

Since I also have a daytime job, I realized there was no reason for me to keep living in that apartment. So the next place I found was in the West Hollywood area, an old army base that was converted into residential units. It was a two-level apartment with two bedrooms. I showed up and met Grant, a good-looking aspiring actor who lived there. At the time, he was living with his girlfriend, but she wanted to move out.

We hit it off immediately. Grant and I watched TV together and hung out, and even though I wasn't around during the day, we had good times together. About a month in, he told me he'd gotten fired—he had been working as a bartender at a nearby country club. "They think they caught me stealing alcohol," he said. "It's bullshit. You're allowed to take home a little bit." And I remember feeling the heat on my neck, because right behind him was a wine rack stocked with high-end wine. I'm not sure why I believed him, but he assured me money wasn't a problem and he'd get another job soon. Sure enough, he had another bartending gig by the next week.

A few weeks later, the two of us went to Best Buy to pick up some cables. I bought a TV because I found one on clearance. I paid for mine in the back of the store, and as we were walking past the checkout, I saw him holding a bunch of cables and a few other things. "Are you going to pay for that?" I asked. He acted like he had forgotten to pay, but you don't forget to pay for something at a store when you're there specifically for that item. That's when I started feeling a little wary about Grant.

One day I got back from work and saw him wearing a checkered collared shirt. "I have one that looks like that," I said. He looked at me and said, "Oh, this is actually your shirt. I put it on." It wasn't something that had been lying around—he would have had to go into my closet to take it out. He never gave me a straight answer about why he was wearing it, only that he was going to wash it and put it back. He was also a dirtbag who didn't treat women well. He was actively cheating on the girlfriend who had moved out of the apartment by going on OkCupid dates with other girls.

Two months or so into our living together, I got a panicked call from Grant. "Dude, we just got robbed," he said. He was panting and hysterical and ranting, and while we were on the phone, I knew something was not right and that he was screwing with me. I was headed to a show, but turned around to go home. When I got there, Grant described how he tried to come in through the back garage entrance like he normally does, but it was chain locked. When he came around the front, the door was open and his television and computer were gone, as was some artwork.

As he was telling me what happened, a cop showed up—an overweight Latina lady who clearly did not care because robberies happened all the time. He showed her a seven- to eight-inch cut in the kitchen window screen and said they must have climbed in through there—even though the screen was on the inside of the glass window. The cop was sitting there being useless, so I asked Grant to show me how exactly they broke in, but he couldn't replicate it. I kept saying that it didn't make sense, but it was awkward with the cop there. I was livid, but at this point, I hadn't even checked my room yet. The cop needed a list of everything stolen for insurance, and I said I'd go look in my room. "They probably didn't take anything from you," Grant said. I wasn't sure how he could assertively say that they hadn't taken any of my things. When I got there, my laptop, handheld camcorder, and backpack were missing, as were my passport and hard drive. There were also less valuable things missing, like a stack of shirts I'd collected over the years and half a bottle of cologne. It didn't seem like things a burglar would take, instead of my TV, which was still there.

I had a hunch that Grant was behind all this—I already thought he was a bit of a klepto after he was fired from his bar job, had tried to steal from Best Buy, and was caught with my shirt—but I couldn't turn to the officer and say, "I found him!" I kept questioning him after the cop left, and asked if his home insurance would cover the things I'd had stolen. He took my receipts but later said that his insurance couldn't help because I wasn't technically on the lease, just subletting. So here I was, living with a guy who I'm 99 percent sure staged a robbery so that he could get money back in insurance. I felt so defeated, but

I never confronted him. Instead, I made plans to move within the next few weeks. We were never able to talk the same way again—we went from buddies to strangers living together.

I'm much more wary of people now—I think I lost a bit of innocence living with Grant, which is probably a good thing. I'm still pissed that he got away with it. I guess karma will take care of him someday. I think he had the balls to steal from me because I wasn't a poor, starving artist. Because we're both in the entertainment business, I've daydreamed that somewhere down the line I'll be in some position to ruin Grant's life without him knowing.

—T, 33 (M)

THE SERIAL ROOMMATE

I USED TO WORK in the advertising world, where we always went out drinking at night in huge groups. One night, my coworker Jane and I realized we both had roommate situations we wanted to get out of—the guy I lived with picked his feet all the time—so we decided to look for apartments together. This was about ten years ago, and we stumbled upon a rent-stabilized two-bedroom apartment for about $1,700 a month on the Upper East Side. My coworker wasn't set on it, but she hadn't been through the whole New York City apartment search craziness before. I didn't care how small it was, I knew we had to take it.

We hadn't worked together for very long, and I didn't know Jane all that well. Living together was very interesting, because she had some eating issues. She often sat in her room and ate fat-free pudding by herself. And she started seeing a therapist because she ate all of my food, and the therapist suggested that we padlock the cabinets and lock up my food so she didn't eat all my cookies in one sitting. I told her that wasn't possible—we weren't living in a prison. I was fine with her eating my food, as long as she replaced it.

She was also very tight with money. We made about the same amount because we worked together; I don't know what she spent hers on—pudding, I guess. When we went to bars she brought little bottles of vodka with her and then only ordered cranberry juice and poured the vodka in. She was a weird girl.

Our office Christmas party was always a shitshow—they even hired a DJ. One year, we all got drunk, and it was on a weeknight and we had to go to work the next day. The next morning, I rolled into Jane's room, still hungover. She looked at me and whispered, "Is he gone yet?" She'd brought a project manager home and hooked up with him, and thought he was still in the apartment.

Jane was always desperate to have a man in her life. She met a guy on Friendster, and they went out and started dating. Then they started having loud sex all the time in our apartment, though he lived by himself. That was when I got fed up and basically kicked her out. From what I know, they got married and it all worked out for her.

The great thing about our apartment was that we became friends with everybody on the floor. It was like *Melrose Place* without a pool. We could walk through the hallways and say, "We're going out, who's coming with us tonight?" It was like a dorm, bizarre but fun.

The day we looked at the apartment, we ran into the guys who lived diagonal to us while they were on the way to the gym, and the woman from the management company introduced them to us. The minute we moved in, we became friends. We ordered a print from Art.com for our wall, and when we came out to go to work the next morning, they'd drawn in a big *F* on the box to make it Fart.com. I'm still great friends with those guys. And then there were two girls across the hall, Rita and Mia. Once I went into work and I had a voice mail from Mia's mother, asking if I knew where she was. I don't even know how she got my phone number. Mia had a crazy boyfriend with a cocaine problem, and his mother told her that he still used her credit card and was ordering escorts and charging it on her card. Rita and Mia's apartment didn't have a dishwasher so they often came and used mine. They were always asking me for toilet paper. And the other room on the floor belonged to a Portuguese guy who always showed up in his boxers and shirt, and in his heavy accent, said, "I bring you wine from my country!" He was ridiculous, but the wine was really good.

There must have been something special about the apartment complex, because through the neighbors who had lived there for several years, we met former residents. I've been at birthday parties with generations of people who have lived in the building. I have a good friend who I met at one of these parties, and though we never lived in the building at the same time, we've become very close. He's in California now, and I see him all the time when I'm there. I haven't lived in that building in five years, and I'm still friends with so many of them.

I had so many roommates—eight over five years—in the apartment that I kept a list. After my coworker moved out, I found a guy on Craigslist. He was somewhat normal—I always got along better with guys anyway. He moved out because his girlfriend got mad that he was living with a girl. I also met roommate number three, Charlie, on Craigslist, and we later realized we had mutual friends. He started to date a coworker of Rita from across the hall. He was working at a college in Queens, and someone went on Match.com and found out he had an active account. Then we found out he had a girlfriend in Queens as well. He had a side coaching gig in Brooklyn, and he had a girlfriend there too. The big joke was, how did he keep the Bronx and Staten Island out of it? He had girlfriends in three boroughs and an online dating profile. We got along great though; I loved living with him.

After Charlie was a girl who worked at a department store as a buyer. She had nothing between her ears, a total blonde. I'm blond too, but I have a brain. She had a forty-five-year-old boyfriend who lived in Seattle. And she had a weird, creepy doll on a wreath she brought back from Germany that she wanted to hang up. I kicked her out eventually because she drove me crazy. I always felt like I had to invite her out, but I didn't want to hang out with her because she was so stupid. Then there was a guy we called Roach. We're still friends, but he had a lot of loud sex. The wall wouldn't stop moving. He moved out because he wanted to live in a bigger place with guys. After him was roommate number six, a Swedish girl who couldn't afford it. Then Evelyn, who was very young and didn't realize how much things cost. She always wore these big cross earrings that freaked out my Jewish friends. And my last roommate was a friend of a friend from Australia. She was the best—I love her to this day. When she moved back to Australia, my friends told me I'd been doing this roommate thing for too long. "It's time to live alone," they said, and that's what I've done ever since.

—G, 34 (F)

THE CABDRIVER

AFTER GETTING MY MASTER'S DEGREE, I moved in with my college boyfriend in New York. He was living in a first-floor four-bedroom apartment, where the other tenants were Karen, a hospital secretary who he was subletting from; Carlos, an illegal Mexican immigrant; and Frank, a white cabdriver. My boyfriend was paying three hundred dollars for the room at the time and got permission for me to move in with him. Our bedroom was on the corner with a window facing the street, and for a while, I naively thought there was an unusually large number of cars backfiring in the neighborhood. Carlos and my boyfriend were friends, and we saw Karen at dinner or on the weekends. But we barely saw Frank—he was around a bit more before I moved in, but we only ever passed each other in the hallway before he shut himself in his room. He lived behind that door and did not socialize with us.

One weekend, we were out on Long Island when we came back to an insane situation: Frank had died in his room overnight. Karen had walked past Frank's bedroom on the way to the bathroom at six in the morning and heard a weird gurgling sound, but he was so reclusive that she didn't do anything about it. By eleven A.M., she noticed a terrible smell coming out of his room. We were all ignorant about death, and the initial comments from the cops and EMTs were that Frank might have choked on his own vomit. This was a guy who came home and went straight into his bedroom with a six-pack of tallboys. He also took ibuprofen for a knee injury, which is apparently bad for your kidneys. And on top of that, Frank had been mugged earlier that week. We never found out from his family exactly what happened—whether it was related to the mugging, or if he had had too much to drink, or maybe a concussion. Karen felt terrible about not doing anything when she first heard something, but what could she have done?

Afterward, the apartment smelled horrible, and we had to wait for so long while the police stayed in the apartment with us. We gave them coffee and cookies while they chitchatted with us and told us that on the weekend, there was only one medical examiner on call for all five boroughs—this was back in the early '90s. The medical examiner came later that afternoon, but the body wasn't removed until the evening by someone else. We were in the apartment the whole time, and the EMTs suggested that we burn coffee grinds on the stove and put vanilla on the doorframe of his bedroom to cover the smell. But between the dead body and the smell, we couldn't sleep there that night, so we went back out to Long Island. I knew we were abandoning Karen, but Frank's father and brother had been contacted and showed up—we didn't know Frank well at all. I think his family knew that he was a bit of a black sheep, that he wasn't very social and had his own problems.

We later sublet Frank's bedroom as well so the two of us could have more living space. We watched TV in there—I guess it didn't bother us that badly, especially after a paint job. It was such a crappy apartment anyway, and impossible to get any repairs done there. We constantly had a leak in our bedroom ceiling, and we kept a bucket handy. The leak eventually wore through the plaster and was like a faucet pouring into our room.

It was hard to fight with the super or landlord because our names weren't on the lease. I asked Karen to withhold rent at one point so that we could get the fixes done. It was then that I saw a bill for the rent, and as far as I could tell, it looked like the total was $927. This meant that Carlos, my boyfriend, and I were each paying $300 for crap while she was only paying $27 a month—no wonder she wasn't helping us fight for repairs. We didn't live there much longer after that. That pissed me off so much that I'm embarrassed to say that I stiffed her the last month's rent when we moved out, because I thought she wasn't paying enough.

—J, 48 (F)

THE WIDOWED ESCORT

IN THE EARLY 1990S, before Craigslist, there was a service in New York called Roommate Finders, where everyone using the organization paid a fee and was prevetted. It was much less efficient, but felt professional and safe. They had an office on Fifty-seventh Street, and I went there to look through binders of people looking for roommates. I interviewed with many of them, and those who didn't pick you called and said, "We've decided to go in another direction." It was like a job interview, and I remember feeling crushed because some of these people were so cool and I wanted to live with them.

When I first spoke to Diane, she told me she was a widow in her thirties and lived on the Upper East Side. The apartment was in a luxury building with a doorman and a semicircle driveway where cars could drop people off. It was very affordable, five hundred dollars a month. But when I got there, she was definitely in her mid-forties or early fifties. The apartment was full of magazines from the '70s and had tons of stuff in it. My room was a barebones, drywalled space with only a bed in it.

I was starting out in publishing and was very excited to get my career going. But all of a sudden, things began to get crazy. I don't know what Diane did for work—she might have been a sales rep for an accessories line, because there were always samples around. We got eviction notices all the time, even though I was paying rent every month. I started coming home earlier at night to try and do some freelance work. One time I came home and the door was double-locked. I was getting agitated because I had a phone call scheduled when Diane finally answered the door wearing a sexy kimono. I heard someone in her bedroom, and if it weren't for my phone call, I would have been a little puckish and stayed in the living room to see what happened. The minute my phone rang and I went to my room to take the call, I peeked out to see what was going on and saw a guy bolt from her room out the door. And yes, there was money on the table.

It was very sad—Diane was clearly turning tricks. Sometimes I came home and she introduced me to her so-called friends, "Bob" or "Stan," businessmen who were presumably going back to their wives in the suburbs. They were very nondescript-looking men in their forties and fifties. I could tell she had been a beauty back in the day—she had an Ann-Margaret thing going on. There were always guys running in and out of the apartment and cash left everywhere. It was very strange, but thankfully I never heard them getting it on. We chatted sometimes but she never acknowledged what was happening. She didn't want to lose that facade with me, but I think she thought I was an idiot who had no idea what was going on.

It did get a bit gross too—I went to the bathroom one night and there was a huge dildo by the bathroom sink. And once I was watching TV and she sat down next to me on the couch bottomless. After that, when friends came over, I told them not to sit on that part of the couch. She was also very spiteful. I had a zit one day, and she called me out on it: "What is that gross thing on your face?" And once I was wearing a vintage dress that a relative had given me, and she said, "Are you secretly rich?"

I think she had been part of the fashion community in a bigger way before and wanted to maintain that veneer.

Diane was very good at keeping up appearances. As far as the world knew, she had an apartment on the Upper East Side with a doorman, and no one needed to know that this was how she was making ends meet. It was a tragic New York story. I never told Roommate Finders the truth—I just wanted to get away from there.

—C, 43 (F)

THE TOP CHEF

I GOT INTO COOKING at a very young age, because my family was in the restaurant business in Montreal. I grew up in the industry and fell into it, and I've never looked back.

I've had roommates my whole life. I went to two different military schools, and one roommate used to sleepwalk a couple of times a month. You never knew when he was acting out his dreams. I woke up one day and he wasn't in the room anymore. I looked for him everywhere, and it turned out he was standing at attention in his full uniform, with his belt buckled and shoes shined, in front of the mess hall. That was our routine every morning—wake up, get dressed, and line up outside the mess hall. Sure enough, he was out there completely alone, and that's how security found him. We later put motion detectors in our room in case he happened to open the door, since it could have been dangerous.

I studied at the Culinary Institute of America in Hyde Park, and afterward traveled and worked in France and Vietnam. Those experiences gave me a good base of French cooking, classic cuisine, and exotic Vietnamese cuisine. Then I worked for a couple of restaurants in New York City, including Le Cirque. In New York, I lived with three chefs from school in a tiny three-room apartment in Astoria—we could high-five each other from our beds.

A few years later, I heard about *Top Chef* because my sister was a fan of the show—she watched *Project Runway* and *Top Chef* when they first came out. She was constantly e-mailing and texting me, saying I needed to watch the show and get on it. At first I was a little skeptical, but I did enjoy watching the show. At that point, I had been in the business for a while and was a bit jaded and looking for something new to do. So I applied, and before I knew it, I was on *Top Chef.*

On the show, the whole crew lived together in a house in Chicago with a great kitchen, big living room, pool table, and Jacuzzi. It was spacious, but we spent very little time actually sleeping, because we were doing a show. There were six people to a room, all on bunk beds—I shared a bunk with Andrew D'Ambrosi, a tall and burly redhead, and we all shared a bathroom. I felt kind of like a child again. It was interesting being thrown back into a situation where you're falling asleep among others, and once in a while there's a snorer or people making sleeping noises. I think the show does that for a couple reasons, partially because they want you on edge a little bit.

I was used to bunk beds because I grew up with one in my room, and I slept in them throughout high school. But I'd forgotten what it was like to live among strangers, with no personal space. As the weeks passed, people started disappearing because they got eliminated from the show. I was there all the way to the end, so I developed relationships and bonded with the others. I was sad to see people leave, especially my bunkmate, Andy, but when contestants left, we took over their rooms and bunk beds. It made sense if a bed was available.

It took some time to adjust to the cameras and the strangers, but I eventually did make friends, though everyone's mind was on the competition quite a bit. I lived in the house for about two months. I enjoyed myself on the show—definitely more than others who took it very seriously. Not much of the living situation gets aired on television, but it really is what it looks like. It was complete chaos, and there was never much downtime.

I later returned to the show for *Top Chef All-Stars*, where I lived with a bunch of guys—Dale Talde, Angelo Sosa, Richard Blais, Mike Isabella, and Fabio Viviani. That was such a fun experience because everyone was returning. We lived in a penthouse in New York that overlooked the skyline. There was a rooftop, and we all played drinking games and had tons of fun. Mike Isabella in particular snored so loudly. I didn't get much sleep to begin with, but it was especially bad when he was in the room. Mike and I both live in the D.C. area, and before he went on the show for the first time, he came to talk to me about *Top Chef*. He was at a crossroads, and I encouraged him to do it. "It'll change your life, you need to go," I said. I didn't know about his snoring then, or I might have been less encouraging.

I was later on *The Next Iron Chef*, which was totally different. It's a really classy show, and they put you up in a big hotel. I had a room of my own and lived like a king. It was a completely opposite situation.

I've lived alone for years now because I can afford to, and because I had so many roommates growing up. Between *Top Chef*, camp, military school, culinary school, and my years in New York, I must have had at least a hundred.

—SPIKE MENDELSOHN, 33 (M), CHEF AND OWNER OF D.C.'S GOOD STUFF EATERY; WE, THE PIZZA; AND BEARNAISE

THE NEWBORN BABY

I WAS SICK OF THE ROOMMATE REVOLVING DOOR and living with irresponsible twenty-one-year-olds when I decided to look for an apartment in Brooklyn—I wanted a clean slate and thought it would be a nice change from Manhattan. I met Emma and Aaron, an engaged couple who had an extra room in their apartment, through Craigslist. They were a little older than I, more mature, and very friendly and nice. People warned me about moving in with a couple, but I figured they were already engaged and had a wedding date set, so they were probably not going to break up. Plus, they'd mentioned that they might eventually move out, so I figured I could score a great apartment and have two friends move in with me later. It had three bedrooms and a great patio that was almost like a second living room when it was warm out.

The three of us got along incredibly well. They were a bit more settled down than I was. When I came home from a book reading or whatever, they often had leftovers, and we all sat around and watched TV. When Emma and Aaron got married as planned at the end of the summer, I wasn't thinking about their next step. I figured kids were far off in the future, and that they'd move into their own place at that point.

Then one day in January, they sat me down and told me they were pregnant. They were freaked out, like any other new parents. I thought I had some time to figure out what I wanted to do as far as the roommate situation. None of my friends in New York had kids, so I didn't know anything about babies or children beyond my basic babysitting knowledge.

As the months passed, I thought that they might move out first. I didn't want them to go, but I figured they'd want to start a family in their own space. I didn't move out immediately because I liked the apartment and the neighborhood, and I loved going out and having my home be a calm oasis. The deciding factor was my dad, who I go to for a lot of practical advice. I wrote him an e-mail detailing the pros (I liked Emma and Aaron as roommates; it'd be great to stay in the neighborhood; I can afford it) and cons (what if the baby cries all night and I have to go to work sleep-deprived?—I was a bit dramatic). And my dad said, "Babies are not like that." I'm the oldest of four, and he demystified it for me a bit. It wasn't as if I would have to take care of the baby all night—the parents were going to be doing that.

At some point I decided, let's see where it goes. I do like children in general, and Emma and Aaron were okay with me staying in the apartment. It might be weird to have a stranger in the house, but on the other hand, it would have been harder for them to find a replacement roommate. They told me they wouldn't leave the baby in the living room, where she'd be very loud, and said they'd try to disrupt my life as little as possible. I think none of us knew what to expect, which is a normal state for new parents. It was a bit awkward to explain to my long-distance boyfriend that I was going to be living with a baby. But thankfully, he understood and respected that I had made up my mind.

In the meantime, I learned about all these pregnancy things—there's a listserv in Park Slope, a neighborhood in Brooklyn, where parents swap their ridiculous designer baby gear. People came by all the time to drop off clothes, and we oohed and ahhed over the tiny clothes, like a Ralph Lauren shirt for the baby. We had a baby shower for Emma in Prospect Park, and it was a beautiful day out and we were so happy—it was one of those milestone moments where you forget there's going to be an actual child to take care of soon.

When the baby was born, my life stayed more or less the same, but my roommates were transformed. I got to see the new-parent experience firsthand, and for the first six weeks, they were like zombies. They were definitely struggling a bit with taking care of the kid. They were doing a great job, but sometimes I came home and there were random dishes left out. Aaron and Emma were super-clean people, so as soon as they started being a little bit dirty—which was still clean by normal standards—I knew they must have been exhausted.

The first time I held the baby was when she was a few days old, and most people don't get that opportunity. One thing I learned was that in the first couple of months, babies are not super reactive because their eyesight isn't well developed and it's hard for them to see faces. After a while, she started to recognize faces and voices, and that became the fun part. After a stressful day at work, I could come home and play with the baby. It was easy for me, because as soon as she started to fuss or wanted to go to sleep, the parents took over and did the hard part, and I went to the movies.

It was the first month after the baby was born when Hurricane Sandy hit. Luckily, we were on high ground, so all we had was a lot of rain. I remember working from home with my laptop and the baby sleeping next to me, and thinking, "This isn't so bad." I didn't have to do anything except watch her so they could take a nap.

I never felt like the de facto babysitter in the house. I might have changed a diaper once, but they were very careful not to disrupt my life. They only asked me to babysit once, because Aaron had produced a documentary that was being shown at a film festival. The baby was two months old at the time, and I was happy to do it. But at the last minute, Emma decided not to go.

I do remember one day when Aaron was up with the baby on a Saturday morning. I was wandering in and out of the living room, getting cereal and making coffee. Though I'd been chatting with him two minutes before, when I walked in again, Aaron was dead asleep. And the baby was sitting up in her high chair, with a look on her face that said, "Hey! Who's going to play with me? Why are the adults asleep?" I dragged the chair into my room so we could hang out quietly, and that's the closest I came to doing any babysitting. When the parents woke up, they were so embarrassed and kept apologizing, but I knew how sleep-deprived they were.

For a roommate who doesn't pay rent and doesn't clean up after herself, she was pretty great. Her crying only woke me up once or twice, and pretty much any roommate in New York will do that to you.

Eventually, Aaron and Emma decided to move to Boston, where his parents were. I got a job in Chicago, where my boyfriend was. I was sad to give up the apartment and say good-bye to my roommates and their baby. I've been to visit them once so far, and got to see her walking a little and saying a few syllables.

In some ways, I felt like living with them was training for when I have kids. I got to see how crazy it gets in those first couple of months, when you're trying to hold it all together and make sure the baby is fed and sleeping. I browsed a lot of mommy blogs at the time, but it's not the same as seeing it unfold in the flesh. It brought home how overwhelming it is to prepare for a baby; there's so much to read, buy, and do. When I have my own children, I'll have to take primary responsibility for them, and that will be a different ball game. I won't be able to hand them off when they're cranky.

—E, 30 (F)

THE POTHEADS

I GREW UP IN BRITISH COLUMBIA, which is known as a pot-smoking province. What most people call "good pot" comes from BC. My friends and I didn't smoke, but we were the rare exception. My first incident living with mass amounts of marijuana happened when I shared a house with five guys. Four of them worked at a bus company, and figured out that a lot of the buses were being used for shipping marijuana. They started intercepting small packages, and discovered that anything that smelled like coffee was probably pot. They brought the pot home, and one day I saw the guys sitting around the kitchen table with a gigantic, fishbowl-size mound of marijuana. I took one look at it and said, "If the cops ask, I don't live here. I live downstairs."

They all laughed at me, but it only took about two weeks for the cops to show up. They'd been in the middle of a sting, trying to intercept pot as it was being transferred between cities in Canada, and had been waiting for this large shipment that never made it to its destination. The cops had checked footage from bus stations and saw my roommates taking it, and told them they needed it back. One of the guys, Nick, had already sold most of it and spent some of the money on a new guitar, so he had to sell his guitar back and try to track down the weed he'd sold. The cops took the package, drove a bus over it to make it look like it hadn't arrived at its destination because it was run over, and sent it on its way. I don't know if Nick got charged with anything or only got a slap on the wrist, but it was crazy.

About three years later, I was living in a ski resort and working as an instructor. I'd moved there with my boyfriend, but we'd broken up, so I found myself looking for a roommate. I was also working retail and in a fine dining restaurant at night, so I got to know a lot of people in the mountains. One of the people I worked with at the restaurant was a guy named Liam, who was about eight years older than me and very snooty—he thought he knew everything about working on the line.

Liam happened to have a room in his place and was looking for a roommate. The rent was decent, but within the first month of living with him, I realized I might not have made the best decision. He was a nice enough guy, but he was odd. He insisted on roasting his own coffee—he roasted the beans in the oven and then ground them up before making any cup of coffee. My friend came over to visit once and spent the night on our couch, and the next morning, Liam, knowing he was on the couch, decided to start loudly roasting his coffee beans and crash pans around the kitchen. And there were several incidents where I came out of my bedroom and found him in front of the refrigerator stark naked.

When the summer came, we all had a lot more free time because they cut our hours on the slopes and at the restaurant. Liam told me that he was going to go work for a buddy over the summer, and while he was gone, his room started to reek. It stank so bad that I couldn't handle it—I wanted to respect his privacy, but something had to be done. So I went into his room, and as I was opening the door, I noticed that there was soil on the floor. And as I stepped in, I started seeing dirty dishes piled up on the floor and realized that the food was flowering, which was where the stench was coming from. When I walked in to get the dishes, there were pot plants everywhere. I'm five foot two, and some of the plants were about my height, and others were at my waist. They were huge and took up a large part of his room. I thought I was being punked—could I really be living in a house where this guy was running his own little grow-op? All of a sudden, the dopey sides of his personality started to make sense to me. I guess he liked pot so much he had to grow it himself. When he returned at the end of the summer, he showed me the five thousand dollars he had made working on a friend's marijuana farm. Needless to say, I didn't stay much longer. It's too bad I'm not a pot smoker and couldn't take advantage of living with these guys.

F, 36 (F)

THE GERIATRIC RETIREMENT HOTEL

I ARRIVED IN SAN FRANCISCO WITH NO JOB, no home, and no friends. When I got there, I stayed in a hostel for three days and e-mailed everyone I knew who had been to San Francisco before. I lived with an acquaintance for two weeks, but her roommate didn't like having a stranger in the house—she got drunk and punched me my first night there. Three weeks in, as I was job hunting, I realized I needed an actual address for my résumé. In my search for a job teaching English, I saw a posting advertising a hotel for foreign students that was cheap and could be rented for nine hundred dollars a month, which included three meals a day in the dining room.

The hotel itself was in an area of San Francisco known for crack dealers and prostitutes, but I wanted to check it out for myself. As soon as I walked in, it smelled like old people. I asked the manager if rooms were available, and he said, "Why? You know everyone here is over seventy years old, right? Are you okay with living with old people?" I told him I didn't have a problem with it. "Okay," the manager said. "We can't discriminate against your age"—I was twenty-seven at the time—"so if you want it, I have a room I can put you in, but at any time, I might need to fill the other bed with a roommate."

My room was two little hotel beds, a window, and a sink that smelled like pee all the time. I think the previous tenant either thought the sink was a toilet or couldn't get down the hallway ten feet to the toilet. I stayed away from that sink while I lived there.

The building also had its own library, with books that were so crappy that no one would steal them. The books weren't even worth the nickel you might get at a donation place for them. But it had wireless Internet, so I hung out there during the day to job hunt. I fell asleep on the lumpy couch once, and woke up to find an old woman hovering over me. She was about to poke me, and when I woke up, she said, "Oh, I'm so glad you're not dead. Sometimes, in this place, I have to check."

Later that night, when I was eating dinner in the dining hall, the same woman came up to me and tapped me on the shoulder as she passed. "I'm so glad you're not dead," she said, and sat down. Another lady sat down later, and the two started mumbling at each other. The waiter came up to me afterward, and said, "Do you know what happened with those two ladies?" I had no idea. "The second lady is jealous of the first because you're the new meat at the hotel," the waiter continued. "She wants to be your girlfriend and was talking shit about the first one."

I eventually made friends with the next-youngest guy in the building, who was fifty-five years old and was staying there while recovering from a heart attack. He told me the waiter was in on it too. "All the waitstaff here are gay," he said. "They want the new me. They don't know if you're here for the old ladies, the old men, or the young men." Later, when the guy was no longer living there but still hanging out once in a while, in a moment of drunkenness he asked me if I wanted to date him. So I guess he was in on it as well.

Within the first week, I met Roger, who shuffled into the library one day and shyly looked at me. I knew right away that if

I nodded in his direction he'd come over, so I did. He sat next to me and told me all about his life—he had been in movies with Elvis and Ann-Margaret because he was in the right place at the right time. He'd also been a professional ballet dancer, but lived in the hotel alone because he had a kidney stone and didn't have family to support him. The next night in the library, he came over and was telling me more stories. As we said good night, his penis fell out of his pants. I didn't think anything of it, because he was so old, and I thought he didn't know how to keep his pants up. It took a day or two for me to realize that it wasn't an accident—just his way of hitting on me. I went to the movies with a staff member once, and afterward, he asked if I wanted to go back to his room with him, which I politely declined.

It felt like the hotel was the kind of place where people go to die. Almost everyone was on Social Security, and a few had regular nurse visits. An ambulance came around once a month for something serious or if someone had passed away. It was great for the people who needed it. If you couldn't get up for your meal, they'd pack it for you and leave it outside your door. They held happy hours on Friday nights from five to six, where you got a watered-down drink, stale crackers, and old cheese, but everyone fought over it like wild dogs. One Filipino guy sang karaoke songs on a little piano. They didn't call it a nursing home, but it was very similar, only cheaper.

They did try to give me a roommate—a Vietnam War veteran in his late fifties—but he wanted to live with someone more his age. I had the room to myself for the month I lived there. I soon came to realize that I could never have my own space at the hotel—my things often went missing in the bathroom if I left them there overnight, and I knew the staff had a key to my room and could come in and out anytime. I've lived in a few places since then, but I do think about the hotel from time to time. If my girlfriend and I moved in there together, it'd only be $1,800 for a downtown location and free food. Maybe we could even pick a room without urine in it.

—T, 34 (M)

THE HOUSEBOY

BETWEEN AN INTERCONTINENTAL MOVE BACK to the States and unemployment, I'm currently in a bit of a quarter-life crisis. I'd been living in Europe for several years when my job contract ended. I had traveled a lot abroad and had great experiences, but was ready to move back to the East Coast. My friend Ben, who I've known since I was twelve, had been telling me for a year that if I ever moved back to the States, I could move in with him and his fiancée, Becca. I stayed with them briefly last Christmas and knew they were looking to buy a house.

This past spring, Ben brought it up again: "If you ever want to move to Philadelphia, you have a place with us." I have a bunch of other friends who live in the city, and I felt a greater draw to Philly than anywhere else. I eventually got Ben to sit down and formalize an agreement: I'd live with him for two months, rent-free, but was expected to chip in on the cleaning, cooking, and other little things around the house, particularly because I was, and still am, unemployed. Becca was completely on board with the plan. She runs a business out of the house, and Ben has a fairly demanding job in the city. The two of them love to eat but don't always take the time to make food for themselves, whereas I love to cook for other people. It was clear that they'd love it if I was around to make meals regularly and cook enough for everybody.

Becca liked the idea of having another person in the house to hang out with, and since I've been close with Ben for a while and she hadn't gotten a chance to spend a lot of time with me, it was a bonus that I lived upstairs. The house is huge. It has three floors with seven bedrooms—two were converted into offices, others include my room, another room for actual guests, and a crafts room—plus three full bathrooms, for the three of us and two dogs. It's big enough that sometimes I can go days without seeing them due to our different schedules. A couple of weeks ago, I didn't see Ben for four days straight even though we live in the same house.

When the two months were up, we sat down to figure out the next step. "I know we agreed on two months rent-free," said Ben, "but you're chipping in more than anticipated. We love having you here, so stay as long as you want." Most of my job description around the house is being a general errand boy. I drive to Home Depot and pick things up for them, because they're doing a lot of home improvement. It works out perfectly, between their work schedule and my lack of one, for me to do things like that on a Wednesday afternoon. I get groceries fairly often, I clean up, I take the dogs for walks. We have a whole e-mail chain of things Becca wants me to look into, such as the type of gravel to put down on part of the yard for the dogs to hang out on. Most homeowners figure that out on their own; Ben and Becca happen to have somebody around with a fair amount of time on his hands who is skilled on the Internet. They've been selling it as, "He bakes fresh bread. What more could you want?" Once a week or so, I e-mail the two of them and ask which days they're around for dinner, and run recipes past them. It's household meal planning, but with three adult tastes. We sit down together about once every week for dinner, whether it's something I made that day or leftovers.

I also help Becca and her business with technical things like IT consulting—the other day, she asked me for help figuring out what type of laptop to buy for her studio. I also call myself the VP of marketing, because I carry around her business cards and constantly meet people socially and professionally. Becca's always looking for clients but rarely on the prowl, so I help her drum up new business.

My friends have a range of opinions. Some have said, "If you ever get tired, you can come stay with us in Pittsburgh or San Francisco." One friend made it clear that she would love it if I came and cooked for her family all the time, but she didn't have room for me. Most people understand, and some even envy the position. After all, I get to live with my friends and hang out with them all the time. It's much better than moving in with your parents, which is the default for this generation and time. My parents know the deal and understand—they want me to be happy. They took it pretty well when I told them I was moving to the States, but not back home with them.

Even though my Ph.D. is in psycholinguistics, we have a hard time coming up with the right language for our situation. There's no good term for the guy who lives upstairs. Becca refers to me as the houseboy sometimes. Ben is my housemate, landlord, friend. We share a living space, but we didn't decorate it together—he did that with Becca. It's been much more fun than stressful.

I can see myself staying in this situation for at least a few more months. I'm still young, but I also don't want their kids to ever say, "Why does Uncle N. still live upstairs?" Culturally speaking, it's not weird for nonrelatives to share a household. It's very much a post-1950s idea of a nuclear family. When you look at all the sitcoms, whether it's Alice as a live-in housekeeper on *The Brady Bunch*, or *Full House*, which is the definition of a family with a lackey uncle hanging around, it's not unheard of. It just wasn't what I was expecting to be doing in my thirties.

—N, 32 (M)

ACKNOWLEDGMENTS

If I could thank each and every person who contributed a story by name, I would. But I've been sworn to secrecy on your identities, so I'll just say, thank you for trusting me with your stories. You are some of the most inspiring, hilarious, and brave people I have had the pleasure of interviewing. I hope I've done your tales justice and that the worst of your roommate days are behind you.

I'm also highly grateful for every roommate I've ever had. From summer camp conversations at lights-out to teaching me how to do laundry or make a grilled cheese sandwich, you've left an indelible mark on my life, allowed me a glimpse into a different culture, and helped me become a functioning member of society.

This book would not exist (or have been nearly as fun to write) without the following people:

Hanya, my fantastic editor, who has taken a million chances on me. Working with you never feels like work—you continuously impress me with your immense talent and infinite wisdom.

Danielle, who has always looked out for me. Thank you for championing me in work and life, challenging me to dream bigger, and showing me that nothing is ever as bad as it seems.

Eimear, for being the guinea pig. Your advice and enthusiasm made it both daunting and exciting to follow in your awe-inspiring footsteps.

Stephen, Peter, Andrea, and the Picador team—this has been the experience of a lifetime, one that couldn't have happened without your patience and guidance. It's been an incredible adventure; thank you so much for bringing me along for the ride.

Mom, Dad, and Alan (my very first roommate)—I'll never be able to thank you enough for the invaluable life lessons, and for everything you've done that's allowed me to do what I love for a living.

And my incredible friends, whose support—from spreading the word to spending hours in coffee shops with me—has been immeasurable. This is by no means an exhaustive list, but here are a few: Ashley, Christine, Denise, Diana, Guido, Justin, Kate E., Kate T., Katie, Laura, Maggie, Marietta, Mary, Meera, Megan, Micaela, Michelle, Nick, Priya, Rachel, Ray, Sam, Vincent, Yo-Jud, and my fantastic colleagues, past and present, at *Town & Country* and *Mochi*.